The Audacity
OF MARRIAGE

10 PRINCIPLES FOR
LIFELONG MARRIAGE

Books by Hasani Pettiford

Wealth Builders: An Economic Program
For African American Youth

Black Thighs, Black Guys & Bedroom Lies

Pimpin' From The Pulpit To The Pews

The 12 Habits of Successful People

The 12 Habits of Wealthy People

The 12 Habits of Healthy People

The 12 Habits of Effective Leaders

Why We Hate Black Women and
Why We Should Love Them

7 Days of Extraordinary Sex

101 Ways To Love My Wife

101 Ways To Love My Husband

The Audacity
OF MARRIAGE

10 PRINCIPLES FOR
LIFELONG MARRIAGE

Hasani Pettiford

THE AUDACITY OF MARRIAGE

Cover Design by: Juliana Nguyen
Editor: Shannon Pruden
ISBN-13: 978-1540305473
ISBN-10: 1540305473

For booking information contact:
Couples Academy
Phone: 678-200-8996 info@couplesacademy.org
www.couplesacademy.org

Discounts on this book are available for bulk purchases. Write or call for information on our discount program.

Contents

Dedication

Abba, Father, You said that if I commit my works to you, you would establish them and make my plans succeed. You are the Faithful One, and I have witnessed that you do not lie. You actually follow through with what you say you will do. So this book is dedicated to you, the Creator of the heavens and the earth.

Danielle, it has been fifteen years since we began our journey together. Little did I know when I first laid eyes on you that you would ultimately become the love of my life. There is no woman on earth whom I admire and am inspired by more than you. You have stood by my side when most would have walked away. You have challenged me to be more, and to walk into the fullness of what God has placed inside of me. Simply said, my life would be on a completely different path void of your life-long partnership.

Paris, Madison, Savannah and Syndey, our beautiful and talented daughters; you are far more than anything we could have hoped for, asked for, or even imagined. Each of you inspires us in so many ways. You are developing into amazing young women who will have a great impact on lives around the world.

My parents, Ralph and Shirley Pettiford, you two have been the cornerstone of my life and have given me the foundation for a long-lasting marriage. Your example as a couple has been a powerful demonstration of faith, love and commitment. Your legacy of faithfulness has securely anchored me in my marriage.

Acknowledgements

This book is the result of years of thought, prayer, and study – and a lot of trial and error. Special thans to those who walke with us on this journey and helped make this book possible.

Danielle Pettiford, my ever-couraging wife, girlfriend and confidant. Our personal journey and joint work with couples have written the pages of this book.

Shannon Pruden, my editor, for helping me get this book out of my head and properly craft the message in a penetrating way.

Juliana Ngugen, my designer, for playing a major role in the cover design and all marketing materials for Couples Academy. You did an AMAZING job.

To the entire Couples Academy Internship Team of the Summer of 2016: Timothy Guzman, Ana Maria, Chazz Wilcox, Shayna Mohanty, Natalie Coke, Kara Lawrence, Becki White, Chris Fernandez, Justine Torres, Lorenzo Williams, Joseph Williams, and Paulina Antillon. Your envolement with the book and Couples Academy is truly immeasurable.

Introduction

Dear friends,

I have a question for you. When you met at the altar and gave your vows, was it your goal to end up in a less than desirable marriage? Did you strive to be emotionally disconnected, unable to communicate, sexually incompatible, financially strained, and in a constant state of conflict? Of course not! No one goes into a marriage wanting marital stress. Like most couples, you probably went into marriage completely in love, thinking that your life and partnership was wonderful. Like most couples, you probably thought your marriage would experience a few bumps and twists, but nothing like what you are experiencing now.

Unfortunately, as Danielle and I travel around the world fulfilling the mission of Couples Academy, we encounter many couples who live in their marriages by default, rather than by design. We meet hundreds of couples living in marital hardship, disillusionment, and conflict. 80% of the couples we meet are miserable. They wear masks in public, giving false impressions to the world that everything is great. I can't tell you how many couples display a grossly distorted view or their marriages on Facebook, posting perfect pictures that express love and compassion, success and wealth. They share their birthday parties, vacations, dedications, heartfelt messages, and otherwise happy times, but hide the real story behind closed doors. They don't talk, argue constantly, have little to no sex, struggle financially, experience betrayal, and live in utterly unfulfilling marriages. Too many couples are choosing to live with their pain and discontent, when they should be seeking help.

Why do so many choose a dying marriage when a solution is readily available? Perhaps they worry too much about their social standing. They're too concerned with saving face, not realizing that when you remain unhappy in marriage, people know. In fact, the strife eats away at you until you are no longer happy. Instead, the misery turns you into someone that no one wants to be around.

Or, perhaps they believe they will miraculously beat the odds by praying and waiting on God. However, it doesn't make much sense to wait on the power of God, when you don't exhibit evidence of a Godly marriage. Most Christians are under the false impression that we are not capable of taking steps toward solving our own problems. The reality is that God doesn't work for us. He works through us. In essence, we must take personal responsibility for our marital situations while we continue to lean on Him. We must pray as if everything depends on God, but work as if everything depends on us.

Or, maybe they are full of pride, refusing to seek help because they believe that they already know what to do. Albert Einstein said, "No problem can be solved from the same level of consciousness that created it." When you do what you've always done, you get what you've always gotten. Continuing on the same path leads to marriages filled with regret and confusion, producing couples who are unsure of how to fix their situations. They have no clue what the end of their path even looks like, let alone how to get there.

Have you ever thought, *If only I knew how to have the marriage I've always wanted...*? Or what about, *If only someone could tell me exactly what to do to be successful in my marriage...*? If you met a truly happy couple who could tell you what to do, or who could give you the secret to marital success, would you listen? Or, would you rationalize how it could never work for you? Would you respond, "We are not the same people we were when we first met"? Or, "We've been through too much to recover"?

Unfortunately, because no marriage is perfect, no single couple has all the answers. However, it is possible to find couples with the knowledge and skills you need. I truly believe Danielle and I are one of those couples. We want to share our knowledge with you. We have navigated the waters of marital discontent, arriving at the island of marital success.

Years ago, I learned that 50% of all marriages end in divorce. Another 30% experience an emotional or social divorce. This means that 80% of all marriages result in some kind of divorce. Only 20% of couples experience a fulfilling marriage. For years, Danielle and I dwelled among that distraught 80%.

Our marriage began like most others. We started out with a professional relationship, which turned personal. We dated for 18 months before we married. Like most couples, we started out madly in love, but after a year and a half of bliss, things began to spiral out of control. There was a period in our relationship that was completely devoid of love, respect, or any interest in moving forward. Our storybook romance had turned into a marital nightmare.

We struggled with major financial hardships, in-law challenges, poor communication patterns, parenting woes, a serious shortage of passion, a lack of conflict-resolution skills, and a major emotional disconnect. Danielle's constant plea for counseling was frequently met with apprehension and disapproval. As our family grew, so did our mountain of issues. Things slowly moved from bad, to worse.

Fortunately, I finally woke up and realized that I was in danger of losing everything- my wife, my family, my reputation, and my entire way of life. It was at that moment that I decided to do something. We had a choice to make. We could remain stuck in the 80%, or we could fight to be in the 20%. We chose to be in the 20%.

Danielle and I enrolled in a self-paced intensive program that changed the trajectory of our marriage. As we learned and practiced the skills required to be successful, things began to change. After countless failed attempts to fix the relationship, we finally learned to look inward. With a renewed focus of working on ourselves in addition to the marriage, our relationship improved drastically. We learned the principles of marital success and lifelong partnership, which made it possible to cross over the bridge from the 80% group into the 20% group. Our transformation gave us a renewed sense of purpose.

We decided to ensure the success of our marriage by getting trained and certified as marriage and family coaches. We have guided many of our clients into the same marital bliss we are now experiencing by embracing and teaching the lessons we were taught. After helping countless couples restore their marriages, we decided to birth Couples Academy. We started Couples Academy because of our personal passion to warn couples that life's road ends in despair, discontent, and divorce without a plan and concerted effort.

Our message has been spread to millions of people all over the world via television, radio, seminars, webcasts, and free training calls at CouplesAcademy.org. Now, we want to share our lessons with you in a more personal way. This book is a way for us to have a long conversation. It is a way for us to coach you on how to have the marriage you have always dreamed about. We can show you how to effectively communicate, express genuine love, experience sexual fulfillment, properly manage your home, overcome financial challenges, resolve conflict, protect your marriage, heal from past hurts, and so much more.

Because you are reading this book, we know you believe there is more to marriage than what you are currently experiencing. We know you want more- not just for yourself, but for your family as well. You can imagine how incredibly freeing it will be when you and your spouse have learned the principles that have given us more fulfillment than we ever thought possible. These principles have helped us in every area of our lives. We now have a great marriage, and we are fulfilling our collective purpose together. We run a successful business, travel the world, and help to save and restore marriages and families globally.

To be successful in marriage you have to be sacrificial, selfless, serving, and forgiving. You have to become something you've never been, in order to be something you've always wanted to be. Marital success is directly related to our personal growth and development. In order to have a successful marriage, you have to be audacious- bold and daring, never giving up. Through this book, we will teach you to become audacious. We will teach you to fight for your marriage. If you are willing to learn, work diligently, and use the strategies offered here and on our website, CouplesAcademy.org, you and your spouse will experience a new sense of freedom and fulfillment. So let us begin. Here it is- *The Audacity of Marriage*.

chapter one

Marriage Is a
GOD IDEA

Finally, the day had come. Twenty-three months after Danielle and I met, we entered into holy matrimony. On Saturday, October 26, 2003, we stood together at the altar to establish our marriage vows. Family, friends, and co-workers came from all over to witness the occasion. We were very well aware that our union would be an unbreakable bond, sealed by a supernatural covenant. We were confident that it would leave a seismic impact on the world that could not be erased.

I stood at the altar in anticipation as Danielle slowly made her way down the aisle, and Daryl Coley's wedding song, *Finally I*, filled the room. It was a song so befitting of our journey together. Finally, our partnership would be cemented before God. Finally, our individual purposes would align to make an impact on the world. Finally, for the first time, we would be able to fully embrace our long awaited expression of love and sexual intimacy.

Though we wrote our own vows, we also recited the traditional vows- to have and to hold from that day forward, for better or worse, in sickness and in health, to love and to cherish, until parted by death. After exchanging vows, the ceremony ended with the minister's final declaration, "And now I pronounce you man and wife." At that moment, our marital covenant was birthed.

The problem with vows is that they are often not valued. Though most know a vow is supposed to be an earnest promise to perform a specific act, they become no more than words spoken with no substantial follow through. Most people do not realize that once vows are exchanged and the marriage is consummated through the act of sex, a threefold covenant is established between both partners and God.

A Covenant, Not A Contract

The covenant established at a wedding ceremony is the most vital component of a successful marriage. It is a binding agreement to be totally committed to someone for life. The only way that God enters into a permanent relationship with anyone is through a covenant. In biblical times, when a covenant was formed, it was sealed through the cutting of flesh and the shedding of blood.

A knife was used to sacrifice an animal, which was then cut into two parts and placed opposite of one another with a space in between. The participants would walk through the path of animal blood, establishing a life-long covenant. As each partner walked through the path of the dead animal, it symbolized the death of each participant unto him or herself. Without sacrifice, there can be no covenant. A death must take place in order for a covenant to be established. Hebrews 9:16-17 says, "For where a covenant is, there must of necessity be the death of the one who made it. For a covenant is valid only when men are dead, for it is never in force while the one who made it lives."

At a wedding reception, couples typically bend and carefully walk through the wedding party line. Occasionally, the best man and maid of honor hold up swords, crossing them at the blade. This wedding tradition is symbolic of a couple entering their marriage by cutting a covenant through the process of death. There's no physical death, but there is a symbolic one. It means that both partners allow their former life to die, in order to create a new life with each other. It means that they are willing to sacrifice their own lives and offer them for the benefit of each other. The marriage covenant, which can be broken only by death, represents the deepest level of commitment on earth. Unfortunately, many of us have lost our reverence for God's first institution.

When you buy a car, it is understood that it will be with you indefinitely, or until its death. However, leasing is a program that allows you to trade the car in for a newer model every three to five years. In essence, if something comes along that interests you, you are given the right to trade in your current vehicle for another. Unfortunately, many people treat their marriages like they treat their cars- if the marriage doesn't meet their expectations or approval, they believe they have the right to trade their spouse in for another model. However, marriage was intended to last until death.

It's interesting that so many of us invite God to our weddings, but refuse Him access to our marriages. We forget that marriage is God's idea. We view this holy union through worldly goggles. It is true that marriage provides a multitude of health, financial, and legal benefits, but there is a greater purpose that God intended for it.

Marriage Reflects the Image and Likeness of God

Marriage is not a human invention, a social construct, or an evolutionary development. Its origins reside in the mind of God. In fact, the book of Genesis gives us a look into the mind and heart of God regarding His plan for the first couple, and all subsequent couples who would come together to populate the earth. The Bible teaches us that Adam and Eve were the first man and woman, the original couple created by God. They represent our forefather and mother, our model and prototype. Everything God wanted a man and woman to be, He put within Adam and Eve. They were the physical manifestation of God's true image. Genesis 1:27 reads, "So God created man in his own image, in the image of God created he him; male and female create he them."

It's quite clear that man is the masculine expression of God's image, while woman is the feminine expression. It is also clear that when man and woman come together, they represent the totality of God's image upon the earth. So, the image and likeness of God on this planet is tied to our human masculinity and femininity. These gender terms are more than a social, political, economic, or feel-good crusade for equality. Gender is one of the fundamental expressions of the image of God, a part of His grand design.

God knew what He was doing when He created us. There is a beauty and wonder to masculine/feminine polarity, interconnectedness, and interdependence that brings the best out in both. One of the biggest challenges in marriage is the total lack of understanding, appreciation, and respect for what is feminine, what is masculine, and what it means to be the counterpoint to the other. Marriage is the joining of two distinct minds, bodies, spirits, personalities, and genders.

Unisex clothing cannot erase the fact that men and women are very different creatures. Each operates as their best selves when they revel in those differences with awe and respect. In order to better appreciate differences in gender, we must identify the best qualities of each group.

In Dr. Laura Schlessinger's book, *The Proper Care & Feeding of Marriage,* she features a comprehensive list of questions. The following are two questions that bring to light the qualities possessed by men and women, which attract us to one another.

Question 1: What do you, as a man, most admire about women in general?

1. Their social skills, nurturing nature, compassion, sensitivity, listening skills, focus on relationships, and ability to bond with friends, family, and community members.
2. Their physical softness and sexy, curvy, beautiful, graceful bodies.
3. Their power to create new life, willingness to sacrifice for family, and ability to be mothers.
4. Their aptitude for details and multitasking.
5. Their ability to take the hard edges off of this world, bringing feelings, emotions, and a sense of intimacy to us logical guys.
6. Their ability to create a home out of any environment by adding aesthetics- color, grace, and beauty- and their ability to make a house into a sanctuary, a home.
7. The positive effects they can have on their husbands and families.
8. The gentle power femininity has over people.

Question 2: What do you, as a woman, most admire about men in general?

1. Their hardiness, physical strength, masculinity, mental toughness, protective nature, courage, self-confidence, perseverance, and emotional strength when facing fear.
2. Their practicality and abilities to see the whole picture objectively, think logically, and get things done.
3. Their honesty, straightforward mentality, strength of character and opinion, and uncomplicated nature.
4. Their ability to get over things fast and become friends with other men who have hurt their feelings; they are not petty, catty, or gossipy, and they bond easily, don't make everything a crisis, are up front with anger, and don't overanalyze everything.
5. Their ability to provide for the family, be responsible and driven to fix and help, and devotion to leadership.
6. Their chivalry, gentlemanly behavior, willingness to slay dragons every day and to sacrifice everything to make their woman happy.
7. Their passion comfort with their bodies; they are put together nicely.
8. Their simplicity.

Typically, we are attracted to our partners because of their differences from ourselves. However, in time, the very things that initially drew us to one another can become the very things that repel us. In our attempts to make ourselves feel good again, we try to fix our partner- make them more like ourselves. Unsurprisingly, this creates more conflict.

Somehow, we forget that there is a reason opposites attract: it's good for us. God intentionally created us different so that completeness could be found in our union.

God created individual expression in each of us, and He gave us an established set of principles to govern that union. With a couple's acceptance of their inherent differences and the proper implementation of God's governing principles, every marriage is designed to excel and be used for God's glory upon the earth. God is so amazing that He established laws to properly govern the unification of the individual uniqueness in our God-given genders. For the purposes of this book, we will only cover two of them.

The first is the Law of Unity. This is the basic law of life. According to the Great Soviet Encyclopedia, The Law of Unity says that any whole, as we see in nature or in a relationship, is a divided system. Each half contains tendencies that are incompatible with the other. If we acknowledge its validity, we might be surprised at just how helpful this law can be. Each part of a unit is a complete whole in itself. For example, atoms are made up of several particles. Each of these particles is complete alone, but they make up a larger unit - the atom.

So, however small any part may be, it must be complete on its own in order to contribute to the greater whole. In this same way, our own wholeness is an essential factor in contributing to a greater whole. As long as we keep in mind the importance of our own individualities building up to a greater whole within our partnerships, expansion as an individual is a good thing. The more we expand by growing spiritually, financially, and educationally with consideration of this greater whole, the more effective we become as units within the partnership. The Apostle Paul perfectly addressed this powerful concept in I Corinthians 12:12-26:

"For as the body is one and has many members, but all the members of that one body, being many, are one body, so also is Christ. For by one Spirit we were all baptized into one body—whether Jews or Greeks, whether slaves or free—and have all been made to drink into one Spirit. For in fact the body is not one member but many. If the foot should say, "Because I am not a hand, I am not of the body," is it therefore not of the body? And if the ear should say, "Because I am not an eye, I am not of the body," is it therefore not of the body? If the whole body were an eye, where would be the hearing? If the whole were hearing, where would be the smelling? But now God has set the members, each one of them, in the body just as He pleased. And if they were all one member, where would the body be? But now indeed there are many members, yet one body. And the eye cannot say to the hand, "I have no need of you"; nor again the head to the feet, "I have no need of you." No, much rather, those members of the body which seem to be weaker are necessary. And those members of the body which we think to be less honorable, on these we bestow greater honor; and our unpresentable parts have greater modesty, but our presentable parts have no need. But God composed the body, having given greater honor to that part which lacks it, that there should be no schism in the body, but that the members should have the same care for one another. And if one member suffers, all the members suffer with it; or if one member is honored, all the members rejoice with it. "

This passage completely rejects the notion that we should live life independent of one another. As married partners, we are individually whole and have a specific function and purpose within our unity, which is essential. God made us different, yet necessary. Our opposites attract and function well when properly understood.

To further my point, upward cannot exist without downward. They are opposites, but each of their existences validates the existence of the other. Therefore, differences are not bad. We need differences. It's the heart of true compatibility. Compatibility is not two people who act, think, and function just alike. Compatibility is represented by two people who share differences that acknowledge, celebrate, and blend together for the betterment of the union. It's making the differences come together that is the difficult part.

All of this may seem like a paradox- the idea that our differences can be challenging and potentially harmful, but at the same time can offer us potential for a more harmonious union. The reality is that everything in creation involves a coexistence of opposing, or differing, elements. When we recognize that our unique individual expression was built into the DNA of marriage, we both win.

The second law is the Law of Gender, which says that all things have masculine and feminine qualities. In marriage, typically one partner is more masculine, while the other is more feminine. It is these opposites- masculinity and femininity- that correlate to the idea of the Law of Unity, that opposites coming together is what brings about transformation. For, without the feminine, the masculine is apt to act without restrain, order, or reason, which results in chaos. The feminine, on the other hand, is apt to constantly reflect, failing to actually do anything, and resulting in stagnation. With the cooperation of both masculine and feminine expression, thoughtful action can breed success.

Sometimes, because of these monumental differences, it is easy to want to leave our partners and move on. However, it is the decision to stick together that helps us learn far more about who we are as individuals than we otherwise would have.

Marriage Is a Three-Fold Cord

As I mentioned earlier, marriage is three-fold covenant between each partner and God. The merging of these three entities represent both horizontal and vertical relationships. The horizontal relationship is the one that exists between a husband and wife. The vertical relationship represents our relationship with God. Together, we form one unit. If either of these components is missing, there cannot be a complete unit. Ecclesiastes 4:9-12 further illustrates this concept of the completion of the marriage unit:

> "Two are better than one because they have a good return for their labor. For if either of them falls, the one will lift up his companion. But woe to the one who falls when there is not another to lift him up. Furthermore, if two lie down together they keep warm, but how can one be warm alone? And if one can overpower him who is alone, two can resist him. A cord of three strands is not quickly torn apart."

This very powerful passage of scripture tells us a number of things. First, God does not want man to be alone, an idea that is reinforced by pointing out, 'two are better than one.' Adam was given Eve as a companion, a helpmeet. The passage clearly illustrates that a partner can be helpful in times of danger and distress, ending with the concept, 'a cord of three strands is not quickly torn apart'. The comparison that Solomon makes to a cord is significant. We see that the strength of three is better than two because, though there are many different kinds of rope, the strongest is comprised of three strands.

Derek Prince, author of *The Marriage Covenant*, also effectively illustrates the power of a threefold rope. He points out that the largest number of strands that can all touch one another is three. If you take away one and leave only two, you weaken the rope. If you add an extra strand and make four, no strength is added because all the strands no longer touch one another. However, with a rope of three strands, if one, or even two of the strands begins to fray, the rope will not break as long as the third strand holds.

In marriage, it is common for partners to become stressed from time to time. They may feel like giving up because of all the pressures that life offers. When you have God acting as the third strand, your rope is not likely to break. While God can remain the foundation of a relationship in all of its seasons, it is only in the marriage season that God actually becomes the glue binding the relationship together. Only in marriage does God become the strand that completes the cord in your relationship. So, no longer are you separate strands; instead, you come together to form the 'oneness' of the cord.

Sacred Marital Geometry

We all know that love triangles are deadly to marriages. However, there is one love triangle that is vital to the success of a marriage. When God is the third corner, a marriage will flourish. To better illustrate this concept, imagine a picture of a triangle with God at the apex and the husband and wife at the two lower corners. If the husband and wife remain at their corners, they are at a maximum distance from God and each other. If the husband moves along the base of the triangle toward the wife, or the wife toward the husband, they get closer to each other, but not closer to God. A move toward your mate, instead of God, is a move in the wrong direction. If both the husband and the wife move along the sides of the triangle toward God, the movement automatically brings them closer to each other. The distance between them closes as they move upward. Increasing their closeness with God increases their fulfillment, and increasing their closeness with each other increases their satisfaction. With this illustration, we can see that God is not an intrusion between the husband and wife; rather, His spirit enables them to love each other. It becomes a catalyst for drawing them together for the closest possible bond.

Also notice in the triangle illustration, both the man and the woman journey toward God on separate paths. Marriage involves two people, each committed to their own personal journey to becoming the fullest expression of who God created them to be. Each journey is unique, with different needs, desires, challenges, and obstacles to address. Each of us is one 100% responsible for our journey. When I stand before the Lord giving an account of my journey toward

Christlikeness, I can't point to my wife and blame her for my failures. Adam already tried that, and it didn't work. Similarly, my wife cannot blame Satan for her shortcomings any more than Eve could have. Each of us is individually responsible for becoming conformed to Christ.

However, great marriages involve helping each other along the way. Though we are completely responsible for our own conformations into the image of Christ, God has given us a companion- a partner- to help get us there. God intends for the companionship of marriage to assist us on our journeys to be like Christ. We feel secure in marriage only when we root our relationship with each other in our relationship with God. When we promise to commit to Him as our source of connection and fulfillment, we bind our mate to our relationship with God.

As Christians, we are called to trust God in all things. Unfortunately, many Christians are excellent at trusting Him in all aspects of their lives EXCEPT marriage. Instead, we justify divorce and make excuses for letting our marriages go. We twist and contort scripture to justify what we want, rather than stand on the truth of God's word. We rationalize separations, arguing that God wants us to be happy. I cannot stress enough how untrue and poisonous these thoughts are. As believers, we are to seek the presence of God in our marriages, while standing firmly on His principles. God's presence allows us to dwell in peace, love, joy, and grace. The proper application of God's principles allows us to establish true success in marriage because, when we truly seek His presence and apply His principles, we experience the fullness of Him in our marriages.

God's Purpose for Marriage

Marriage is far more important than we may have originally thought. The institution of marriage affects God's reputation and fulfills His ultimate agenda for this planet. The Bible tells us in 2 Corinthians 4:4 that **Satan is the god of this world and he has blinded the minds of those who don't believe.** This indicates that he is the major influence on the ideas, opinions, goals, hopes, and views of the majority of people. His influence encompasses the world's governments, commerce and trade, entertainment, educational institutions, philosophies, and culture. So, the majority of this earth is under the control of the Kingdom of Darkness, as Satan rules over the world and its people. As believers, we have the kingdom of God inside of us. God's plan for His kingdom is for it to spread throughout the entire earth.

The bible clearly states that, as believers, we are IN this world, but not OF this world. We are citizens of heaven who have come into this foreign territory called earth as ambassadors of the Kingdom of God. We don't come to take sides, but to take over. We come to dominate this territory for God and make it just like heaven. This assignment is fulfilled through our marital covenants. How, you may ask? Well, marriage is the smallest unit of a nation. Marriages form families, which make up communities, which create nations. A nation can only be as healthy and as strong as its marriages. Also, marriage is the foundation for reproduction- the development of strong future generations. Therefore, a nation is a direct reflection of its marriages and families. God gives three mandates for Christian marriage:

1. A Christian marriage should reflect God's image and likeness.
2. A Christian marriage should rule, have dominion, and spiritually influence the nations.
3. A Christian marriage should produce Godly offspring and replenish the earth.

This plan is clearly spelled out in Genesis 1:26-28:

"And God said, 'Let us make man in our image, after our likeness: and let them have dominion over the fish of the sea, and over the fowl of the air, and over the cattle, and over all the earth, and over every creeping thing that creepeth upon the earth. So God created man in his own image, in the image of God created he him; male and female created he them. And God blessed them, and God said unto them. Be fruitful, and multiply, and replenish the earth, and subdue it: and have dominion over the fish of the sea, and over the fowl of the air, and over every living thing that moveth upon the earth'."

The Genesis account shows us that God wants us to be successful in marriage so that we may reap all of its benefits. It also shows us that Satan and his kingdom will be overthrown and replaced by a new governing power: The Kingdom of God. Wow! What a revelation! If we completely surrender our marriages to the will of God, it will help tear down Satan's kingdom. That's why the devil attacks marriage so forcefully. He uses miscommunication, offensive behavior, unforgiveness, financial hardship, adultery, divorce, and a host of other things to tear marriages apart. He understands what most of us have not yet realized- the divine fulfillment of our unions threatens his kingdom.

Keep in mind, God loves marriage. In fact, He loves it so much that He established it as the first institution on earth. It's even older than the church. God's first covenant was through marriage. It is befitting that Jesus's first miracle was performed at a wedding ceremony. When we begin to understand the purpose and power of marriage, we will become an unstoppable force that no man or power can tear apart. We will recognize that our spouses are not here to hurt or hinder us. They are here to help us fulfill God's purpose for our lives. Only when we come together as couples, seeking his presence and applying his principles, will we be able to cease all power struggles, transforming into power couples. Only when we operate from a position of power, can we dominate the earth and impact all of its nations for God.

Johnny Enlow's book, *The Seven Mountain Prophecy,* explores the idea that there are seven spheres, or mountains, of societal influence:

1. Business
2. Government
3. Media
4. Arts and entertainment
5. Education
6. Family
7. Religion.

God has commissioned us to rule over the earth. Therefore, as power couples, we must strategically choose the spheres on which we have the most influence. Danielle and I formed Couples Academy several years ago because we decided that we were going to become champions for family. So, we are fulfilling the mandate of God by influencing marriages and families worldwide. Which mountain or sphere of influence will you infiltrate and dominate?

God commanded us to be fruitful and multiply-replenishing and subduing the earth through pro-creation. We were created to be creators. He gave us the ability to reproduce Godly descendants. In fact, Malachi 2:15 says, "Did he not make them one, with a portion of the Spirit in their union? And what was the one God seeking? Godly offspring."

We are instructed to train up our children to reflect the character of God, enabling them to influence the next generation. We must impart a sense of destiny in our children so that the kingdom of God will remain forever. Marriage is often a mystery, but the more intimate we become with God, the more revelation we receive. Likewise, the more we know, the more audacious we become.

Couples Testimonial from
Abdul & Yasmin Aziz
Dubai, United Arab Emirates

Getting married was a big step for me and I wanted to know that i was prepared for my life to change. I wanted to know how to effectively communicate, meet each others emotional needs and fulfill each other sexually. I wanted to make sure that we were doing things the right way so i sought out Couples Academy online. They information and perspective was new to us and very enlightening. They have helped us get through some tough circumstances. We now have a great foundation for a life long union.

chapter two

Help: My Mouth is
KILLING
My Marriage

Does your mouth ever get you into trouble? Do you keep saying the wrong things at the wrong times? Does your tongue kill instead of heal? If so, you may be guilty of being a verbal assassin. Verbal assassins are trained killers, responsible for the systematic elimination of opposing figures, often for private gain or compensation. Many verbal assassins have been involuntarily trained since childhood to naturally display their lethal abilities as adults.

A verbal assassin is a vicious murderer who harvests an uncanny taste for blood in his or her mouth. They are hit men and women with an unruly desire to seek and destroy anyone or anything in their path. They have a private arsenal of verbal weapons to fulfill one single agenda: to steal, kill, and destroy a person's joy, peace, self-worth, and life. Their most common verbal assaults involve yelling, threatening, temper tantrums, name calling, and constant criticism.

Verbal assassins are mean, belittling, critical, sarcastic, nagging, disrespectful, fault-finding, intimidating, sharp-tongued, disrespectful, lawless, offensive, cynical, poisonous, and harsh people. They specialize in tearing others down in order to build themselves up. They are always on the defense, ready to fight and argue with anyone who challenges their own self-absorbed, egotistical world view. They love to play devil's advocate, even when they agree with you. They possess a fervor for debating. It is the life-blood running through their veins. Whatever you say, they will say the opposite; if you say, "What a beautiful day it is today," they will search for a cloud, simply to forecast rain. They may not believe that they are always right, but they do believe that you are always wrong, and they will build a case to prove the error of your ways.

Verbal assassins are critical, judgmental people. They often ignore or degrade another person's opinions, advice, or beliefs. They create jokes about other people's weaknesses or shortcomings with sarcasm and cutting remarks. Verbal assassins often subject others to long and reprimanding lectures, treating them like children. They are unwilling to admit their wrongdoings, never apologizing for the things they have done to offend others. Romans 3:13-14 offers an accurate description of these assassins:

"Their talk is foul and filthy like the stench from an open grave. Their tongues are loaded with lies. Everything they say has in it the sting and poison of deadly snakes. Their mouths are full of cursing and bitterness."

I am able to describe the verbal assassin so well because I spent the first few years of my marriage operating as one. I developed a supreme mastery in the art of destructive language. Even before Danielle and I became husband and wife, she witnessed my genocidal onslaught of verbal terror. Many around me including family, friends, innocent bystanders, restaurant servers, customer service representatives, and sales associates suffered my wrath. I looked at Danielle through critical eyes, showing no respect for her perspective. I devalued her opinion, criticized her in public, and barked at the slightest request. Though she'd had a front-row seat to my antics, she remained committed to walking down the aisle and saying, "I Do!" While she was very concerned about my behavior, she had also witnessed a lighter side. She recognized that there had also been many instances of me complimenting, encouraging, supporting, empowering, and uplifting her.

The saddest part about this is that I had no idea of the harm I was causing. Danielle would often complain about my tone and temper, but I refused to change. I was completely oblivious to my destructive behavior. Over the course of several months, I succeeded in crushing her spirit. In the midst of an argument, I realized the impact of my wretched ways. Danielle said that my words were so painful that they "decliterized" her. This word, which is the feminine form of emasculation - depriving a man of his strength, castrating him - doesn't exist as far as the English language goes, but I knew exactly what she meant when it came out of her mouth. In essence, I stripped her of her femininity and womanhood with my words. I was shell-shocked, dumbfounded, and gob-smacked. It led to one of the worst fights we'd ever had. Both of us were in rare form.

After twelve rounds of verbal sparring, we both left the ring, retreating into our corners to recover. Though there weren't any physical blows, then or ever, we both left pretty banged up. My heart was heavy, my adrenaline was high, and my larynx was sore from screaming so loud. It was time to withdraw. Then, just as I thought the worst was over,

Danielle came back in to land a well-timed TKO, saying, "I DON'T CARE ANYMORE! YOU GO AHEAD AND DO YOU BECAUSE I'MMA DO ME!" At that moment, I knew I was at risk of losing her forever. I made an internal vow never to criticize her again and that was the beginning of a new chapter for us.

Stonewalling

We are all familiar with the old nursery rhyme, "Sticks and stones may break my bones, but words will never hurt me." Well, Danielle specialized in taking my stones and building walls with them. Much like the Great Wall of China, she built an impenetrable wall around her that completely shut me out. The purpose of the wall in China was to create a safe society that protected its people and territory from the invasion of nomadic tribes. I was Danielle's nomadic tribe.

She built up that wall, then completely shut down. It was as thick as a six-lane highway, an impenetrable fortress with watchtowers and armed soldiers holding fiery darts, ready to strike. It was surrounded by a moat filled with water and viscous alligators, ready to attack. The gatehouse had murder holes armed with men ready to unleash boiling water at the first sight of an attacker. All of my attempts to scale her wall simply made me a sitting duck.

Everything I said to her was interpreted as hurtful, frightening, threatening, or infuriating, even when it wasn't meant that way. She became extremely defensive, which made it impossible for her to listen to me. Every word I spoke triggered hurt feelings, anger, or fear. This only activated her defensiveness and blocked understanding. She became thin-skinned and sensitive, which caused her to become defensive or angry. At times, all she could do was counterattack or withdraw, making listening the last priority on her emotional agenda.

Another word to describe her behavior is *stonewalling*. Stonewalling is when a listener withdraws from an interaction by getting quiet or shutting down. It creates an obvious silence that feels very uncomfortable. Stonewalling can include the refusal to give nonverbal communication cues, walking out in the middle of a discussion without warning or explanation, avoiding talking about feelings, or explicitly refusing to discuss the issue at hand. This tactic can be distressing when the other partner does wish to discuss an area of conflict, and the lack of communication often causes extreme anger and frustration. Typical phrases made by stonewallers are, "Just leave me alone," "Do whatever you want," "I don't care," and "This conversation is over."

Stonewallers know that silence, the cold shoulder, or emotional isolation hurts their partner. Stonewalling is often a tactic used to gain leverage or power. Because conflict is so overwhelming to stonewallers, they feel that their only choice is to shut everyone out altogether. It took a looooong time for Danielle's wall to come down. By the grace of God, it eventually did.

Shut Up and Just Listen

When conflict arises, people typically have two very distinct communication styles. There are *peacemakers* and *peacekeepers*. Peacemakers are those who want peace at any cost. Ironically, they will go to war in order to preserve the peace. They prefer to face conflict head on, resolving it faster, thus making peace faster. Peacekeepers, on the other hand, desire to keep the peace as often and for as long as possible. They are conflict avoiders and their answer to conflict is to sweep it under the carpet. When two people disagree, the peacekeeper will make every effort to postpone conversation until later.

By now, you should have a pretty good idea of how bad a communicator I was. Well, guess what? My listening skills were ten times worse. Not only did I excel at verbally attacking Danielle, I was a world-class champ in the fine art of interrupting. The only person that I could stand listening to for long periods of time was me. Why? Because I was always right. When you're always right, listening to anyone else is a waste of time.

In my warped mind, Danielle's strange opinions had little merit. I second guessed her logic and devalued her feelings. Taking the time to listen with intent was the last thing I wanted to do. The only thing I can recall hearing Danielle say again and again and again was, "Let Me Finish!" After years of hearing me offer up weak apologies for the same behavior, she eventually got fed up and became just as belligerent as I had been. Rather than allow me to cut in, she would railroad me with her words in order to finish her point.

This verbal dance went on for quite some time, until things got really bad in our marriage, and I realized I had another mountain to climb. It was called *effective listening*. In time, I realized that listening is one of the most powerful forms of communication known to man. It has two purposes:

to take in information and to bear witness to another's thoughts and feelings. To listen means to pay attention to, care about, acknowledge, appreciate, and take an interest in what our partner says. In relationships, we often hurt each other by failing to listen to and acknowledge each other. Not being listened to makes us feel ignored and unappreciated, cut off and alone. However, being listened to makes us feel that we are taken seriously, that our ideas and feelings are known, and that what we have to say matters.

You might catch yourself rehearsing what you're going to say next while your partner is talking. Unfortunately, simply holding your tongue while the other person speaks isn't the same as listening. To really listen, you have to suspend your own agenda, forget about what you desire to say next, and concentrate on giving your full attention to the other person. Listening is a learnable skill that is within everyone's reach. Just as your eyes can be taught to see more clearly, your ears can be taught to hear more clearly. Most people are under the impression that, by listening, we place the other person in control of the conversation. However, nothing can be further from the truth. The listener, not the speaker, controls the conversation.

Compare listening to driving a car- the person talking is the engine and the person listening is the driver. The engine provides the power, but the person at the wheel decides where the car will go. You, the listener, can give direction, guiding the flow of the conversation with the statements you make and the questions you ask. One form of active listening is called paraphrasing. When you paraphrase what another person is saying, that person will continue to talk. Likewise, when you verbally agree with the talker, you encourage them to share even more.

Initially when listening, the speaker may talk even more, but if you remain perfectly silent, you create such tension within them that they begin to simmer down. I'm not talking about using the silent treatment, which is an unfair weapon that will destroy a relationship. I am saying that, by not responding, you let the other individual know that you are through with your part of the conversation. Your silence points to the fact that true communication is a give and take process. However, there are rules to give and take communication.

In order to engage in effective listening, it is important to remember not to interrupt. According to *The Complete Idiot's Guide to Etiquette*, interrupting is the most common, and one of the most irritating errors people make in conversation. It's hard, but not impossible, to overcome. Like any other bad habit, not interrupting others requires reworking the way we look at the situation and re-training ourselves within it.

Being rudely interrupted in a conversation can be severely annoying, but what if you are the one who typically does the interrupting? The best way to avoid cutting someone off is to concentrate on what he is trying to say. Give him a chance to make their point. Acknowledge it, meditate on it, and then give your response. Don't dive in at the first pause. Let the other person finish, then give him a chance to exhale and collect his thoughts before jumping in. Stop and consider whether your comment contributes to the conversation or disrupts it.

Interruptions are typically motivated by assumptions that are made. For example, assuming you know what someone is going to say means you don't have to bother listening. There is a certain level of arrogance exhibited when one refuses to grant another the privilege of expressing her thoughts and feelings. It's dismissive. The essence of good listening is empathy, which is achieved by being receptive of what other people are trying to say. Empathy requires opening your mind to other sensibilities. Even if you do know what the other person is going to say, he or she still deserves the chance to say it, have you listen, and then have you acknowledge it so that they may feel understood. So, the next time you feel the urge to interrupt someone, DON'T!

Secrets, Lies & Dishonesty

Shhhh, there are certain secrets that you should never tell. Right? Well…no. Where secrets dwell, deception is conceived, and lies are birthed. Relationships are comprised of people who wear masks, hiding behind false faces. Initial interactions start with lengthy phone calls, romantic gestures, special dates, and lots of time spent getting to know each other. Then, after feeling totally comfortable and ready to offer your heart, "Wham!" A bone falls out of the closet of your partner's past. Comfort is lost as tension arises. While crushing revelations roll off of the tongue of the confessor, intense feelings of disgust and betrayal begin to sift through the recipient's mind. His heart starts to palpitate. His eyes begin to squint with rage as silent tears roll down his face. A loud, deafening silence fills the air.

How did this all start? It started with one secret, shamefully covered up by just one word- a lying word, full of deception. It started with one word that hid the iniquities of the past. Perhaps it was a secret about children, a previous relationship, or financial status. Whatever they may be, untold secrets can destroy relationships. It is believed that some things are better left unsaid; however, in a secure relationship, each mate should feel confident enough to discuss issues of a sensitive nature with respect and tact. If a secret is relevant to the present relationship, the truth must be told. Most people don't tell really intense secretes until they have reached a point at which they feel safe and secure in the relationship. This point is hardly ever in the beginning, but the sooner sensitive matters are discussed, the better. It is better to speak the truth than to live with the fear, deceit, and shame that comes from hiding the truth from your mate. Though confessing may potentially risk the security of the bond, in the end the relationship will be much stronger if you are dealing with a fairly balanced person.

Often, the biggest lesson people must learn is that when you marry someone, you are marrying their past, present, and future. It's important to know as much as you can about that person. So, if you are someone who believes: (A) You never tell your spouse everything, (B) What a person doesn't know won't hurt them, (C) They're better off not knowing, or (D) Things that happened before I met my spouse don't matter, you should tell that to your banker the next time you apply for a loan.

Mention that to the employer of the next job you apply for. See how far it gets you with the next home that you attempt to purchase. Before a banker, a loan officer, a landlord, or an employer will make a commitment to you, they will require you to complete their paperwork. They will pull your credit, check your references, take your blood, do background checks, and a whole lot more. If you were to tell them your past is not important, they would laugh you right out of their offices. So, if it is important to them, how much more important is it to someone you will share the rest of your life with?

To feel secure, a person must trust his or her partner to provide accurate information about the past, present, and future. For instance, what you have done? What you are thinking or doing right now? What plans do you have for the future? For this reason, I subscribe to the concept Dr. Willard Harley Jr. has coined as the *Policy of Radical Honesty*. This policy is defined as revealing to your spouse as much information about yourself as you know, including your thoughts, feelings, habits, likes, dislikes, personal history, daily activities, and plans for the future. It is broken down into four parts, including:

1. Emotional Honesty- Reveal your emotional reactions- both positive and negative- to the events of your life, particularly to your spouse's behavior.
2. Historical Honesty- Reveal information about your personal history, particularly events that demonstrate personal weakness or failure.
3. Current Honesty- Reveal information about the events of your day, your schedule, and your activities.
4. Future Honesty- Reveal your thoughts and plans regarding future activities and objectives.

Radical honesty is hard for most people, including professional counselors. Many believe that dishonesty, limited information, deception, and outright lies are beneficial in certain instances. Granted, dishonesty may look like a good short-term solution to relational conflict. It will probably get you off the hook for a few days or months, or keep the problem on the back burner. It is, however, a terrible long-term solution. If you or your partner expect to live in love and harmony, dishonesty can get you into a great deal of trouble.

While there may be numerous reasons for dishonesty, there are generally only three major reasons for dishonesty in relationships: (1) to protect your partner from a truth that may hurt them, (2) to avoid trouble or backlash that may occur once the truth is revealed, and (3) someone is a compulsive liar. While these motives are very different from each other, the result is the same- the relationship suffers. As you can see, dishonesty puts a real strain on relationships and as the ole' saying goes "Honesty is the best policy."

He-Talk, She-Talk

A few years ago, a couple came into my office to begin counseling. They were struggling with an assortment of issues, though the most challenging was communication. The newlywed wife's major complaint was that they never talked. I rarely buy into absolute statements like *always* or *never*. It usually winds up being an exaggeration of a larger truth. However, in this case, I actually believed it because the entire ninety-minute session was spent talking to the wife, while the husband sat with his head pointed down at the floor. If I were a betting man, I would say that he spoke approximately 180 words all night. Though this was an extreme case, many couples do struggle with having nothing to say.

During the dating season of a relationship, talks are endless. Countless hours are spent on the phone. Conversations last into the wee-hours of the morning. Just the sound of your loved one's voice is enough to get you through the day. Many couples even fall asleep on the phone just to remain in each other's company. Then normalcy sets in and everything changes. We begin to struggle to have the same level of intimate conversation we once had. While the reason may be attributed to the loss of novelty in the relationship, gender also plays a role.

There is a gender difference when it comes to talking. Some experts say that women need to speak 25,000 words a day, while men need only 10,000 a day. Most men tend to use up their 10,000 words at work talking to customers, co-workers, or an occasional friend, leaving them with little to say once they get home to their wives and children. Meanwhile, wives using the same number of words all day can't wait to talk- they've got another 10,000- 15,000 words left to go.

While I'm not quite sure how accurate these gender word counts are, it bears mentioning that women generally speak in paragraphs and men speak in bullet points. She's mastered the art of speaking in great detail, while he's mastered the science of summarizing his experiences with short words and phrases.

Another difference between men and women when it comes to talking is related to stress. A woman de-stresses by talking, though she doesn't necessarily want her husband to fix her problem. She feels better merely by verbalizing her feelings. A man, on the other hand, finds talking stressful. He de-stresses by being quiet- doing quiet activities such as watching television. As John Gray, author of *Men are from Mars, Women are from Venus* puts it, men de-stress by going into their cave, a quiet zone in their house, where they prefer to be alone. Of course, whenever we discuss gender differences, there are always exceptions to the rules. In some relationships, the man may be the talker and the woman is the one who prefers quiet. Generally speaking, however, a woman desires to talk more than a man does.

Awareness of these issues is the first step in bridging the gap between a husband and a wife. When partners understand these differences, a man can learn to talk with his wife more, openly sharing some of his feelings. Likewise, a woman can learn to be respectful of her husband's need for quiet and space to de-stress.

Unfortunately, beyond the gender communication differential, it is a reality that too many couples run out of things to say to each other. We often engage in very basic, impersonal conversations that are considered small talk. It's often just enough to avoid being totally disconnected from our spouse. These conversations generally focus around the kids, work-related issues, bills, and household responsibilities.

It's sad to report, but the average couple spends approximately 5 minutes a day communicating. That's not only scary, it's disheartening, especially knowing that we spend 7-8 hours a day communicating with co-workers. We are forming stronger bonds with people outside of our homes than with those inside. I can remember many days that I spent on the road, traveling across the country, speaking to thousands of people, or in my office conducting counseling sessions all day long, talking. Once I was done, I had nothing to say. Danielle would say, "You can talk to everybody else, but you run out of words when it comes to me. I guess you've used up all 10,000 of your words, huh?" My typical response would be, "My bad...let's talk. What do you want to talk about?" Danielle would then reply with, "I don't know. What do YOU want to talk about?"

Does this dialogue mirror what goes on in your household? If so, you are not alone. There is another gender lesson here. Generally speaking, men like to bond and women like to connect. When men get together, they bond through shared experiences such as watching a game or playing pool. When women get together, they talk from the moment they step into the room until the moment they leave because they use communication as a way to connect.

Husbands are looking to bond with their wives, while wives are looking to connect with their husbands. This presents a problem because each desire is different, requiring us to show up in completely different ways. So, how do we successfully overcome all of these communication challenges?

Lord, Teach Me How to Talk

The biggest issue couples struggle with when they come into my office is their inability to communicate effectively. In marriages, couples often feel disrespected, misunderstood, taken for granted, and violated. They've lost hope and are looking for a breakthrough.

In the early years of my practice, I counseled an out-of-state couple via skype. They had a major conflict break out during our session. As grievances were expressed, harsh words, disrespectful tones, and insults flew across the room like missiles on a battlefield. Within moments the argument transitioned into a physical altercation. With several unsuccessful attempts to calm them down, things got worse. Threats were made, objects were thrown, and clothes were torn. Before I could regain control of the room, the computer screen went black. We were disconnected. I sat there, waiting in angst. Minutes felt like hours as my multiple call attempts were neither answered nor returned. If I could have flown several hundred miles to be at their doorstep in time to diffuse the fight, I would have. Unfortunately, that was an impossibility, so I was forced to wait. Finally, my skype app rang. The wife sat there, looking despondent on the screen. When I anxiously asked her what had happened, all she could say was, "All of this started over cross words."

As I mentioned earlier, "Sticks and stones may break my bones, but words will never hurt me." Well, we now know that's a lie. Sticks and stones will break your bones, but words will kill you. Words will do what sticks and stones cannot, so it is imperative to learn how to effectively communicate. The fact of the matter is that there is an art and science to effective communication. It is not a one-dimensional exchange of words. Rather, there are three fundamental components to delivering a message.

1. Words (what you say): Our words represent 7% of our communication. Sadly, most people think they are great communicators because they have a large vocabulary and can clearly articulate their perspective on things. However, the art is in knowing what words to use. Harsh, mean-spirited words can become daggers that cut into a spouse's heart, leaving

irreparable damage. Proverbs 12:18 says, "The words of the reckless pierce like swords, but the tongue of the wise brings healing." So, it is critically important to think before you speak, choosing your words carefully.

2. Tonality (how you say what you say): Our tonality represents 23% of our communication. I'm sure you've head the saying, "It's not what you say, but how you say it." No matter how truthful our statements may be, we lose effectiveness if the message isn't delivered in the right way. If we don't learn to tone down, our partners may tune out. Therefore, our delivery must be carefully crafted. Colossians 4:6 says "Let your conversation be always full of grace, seasoned with salt, so that you may know how to answer everyone." Just as food is pleasant to the mouth, words should be pleasant to the ear. We all know how frustrating it is to not be listened to. How many of us stop to think that there might be something about the way we express ourselves that makes others deaf to our concerns? So, ask yourself what message your tone is communicating.

3. Non-Verbal Communication (facial expressions, body language, and gestures): Our non-verbal communication is 70% of our communication. It conveys a message just as our words do. It is possible to say all the right things and still deliver the wrong message. While feelings may not be expressed verbally, they can leak out and morph into body movements. This often happens without the

individual being aware. Rolling our eyes, taking a deep sigh, or crossing our arms can demonstrate signals of disrespect. We must be careful.

When I first discovered these communication components several years ago, I was relieved and overwhelmed all at the same time. Even though it was a lot to take in, I finally understood what Danielle had been experiencing for years. It was at that moment that I began to empathize with her struggle and I began my journey of recovery.

The three aforementioned components can easily convey different messages. The key is getting them to line-up so that your message is properly received. After multiple failed attempts, lots of reading, and some serious self-analysis, I began to understand the rules of effective communication and how to utilize them within my marriage. As each day passes, we continue to do the necessary work required to enhance our communication. And that is our hope for you as well.

Couples Testimonial from
Chris & Keisha Johnson
Atlanta, Georgia

After 6 years of marriage we thought that we worked out all of the kinks and because we were still smiling and functioning that everything was near perfect. Couples Academy gave us the tools to make our marriage more enjoyable. It feels alive and not routine. We feel torn, do we share what we've learned with others, or are we spoiling whatever couples need to experience for themselves? It's like we have a secret recipe for marriage magic. This was the best investment we've ever made in our marriage, and we will continue to put money in our marriage stock because, thanks to Couples Academy, our value is soaring. Thank you for a life changing weekend, we wish it were longer!

Place Your Marriage On The Path To Fulfillment
With CouplesAcademy.org

chapter three

Resolve
CONFLICT
In Your Marriage

Conflict is common in all marriages. Danielle and I have certainly had our fair share of conflict. In fact, we could write a book on what not to do. Oh wait, this *is* that book. When you find yourself stuck in a pattern of discord, unable to resolve issues, it doesn't take long before you can no longer stand your spouse. Therefore, learning how to resolve conflicts in the right way is key to having a strong marriage. Unfortunately, countless marriages are on life support.

I compare marriage to the human body because there are many things that can cause its death. Divorce (marital death) is caused by prolonged unresolved conflict. Even after my many years of working with couples, I am still amazed at the things that cause the most conflict. Often, what is miniscule for one is detrimental for another. Many couples have sat in my office and cried, screamed, thrown things at each other, and stormed out of the room for a multitude of reasons, topics of disagreement often include child rearing, nutrition, dress code, choice of friends, entertainment, drugs and alcohol, household responsibilities, sex, financial decisions, in- laws, work schedules, life decisions, and extra-curricular activities. There really is no limit to the number of challenges, problems, and conflicts a couple may endure. Typically, these conflicts are birthed from two places: differences of perspective and an unwillingness to make necessary adjustments.

Our individual perspectives are often shaped by religion, culture, ethnicity, gender, family upbringing, or past experiences. We collect beliefs throughout our lives that influence how we interpret things. When two people who have had very different life experiences come together, conflict can occur if they both remain unmovable. Much like meat is soaked in a marinade for several hours to enhance its flavor, we get soaked in our own family marinades. Throughout our individual upbringings, we have been soaked and saturated in specific communication styles, patterns of behavior, and unique philosophies and perspectives on life that shape how we interact with others as adults. These very unique marinades need to strike a balance and synergize with our partner's or conflict can quickly arise.

Compromise Is a Curse Word

When couples first come into my office, I take them through a series of questions. I'm looking to identify personal philosophies, life lessons, ministry teachings, and general principles by which they govern their marriages. One of the themes that always comes up is *compromise*. It's quite apparent that most people are taught that they must compromise in order to make a relationship work. At that moment, I take out a sign with a list of curse words that we never use in our office. Comprise is one of the words on that list.

While compromise may have short-term benefits, the long-term implications are devastating because it creates a win-lose scenario. Either you take a loss in order for your spouse to win, or you win at your partner's expense. Either way, someone wins and someone loses. This win-lose paradigm becomes the primary way of resolving conflict for most couples. Then, when conflict occurs, there are a few unproductive responses that follow.

The first unproductive response is that of the loser. He typically suppresses his thoughts and feelings in order to accommodate his spouse's wishes and desires. Suppression is often a coping mechanism that we use in other areas of our lives, such as with our health concerns. For instance, if you have ever suffered from a headache, you have probably been instructed to take a pain reliever to suppress it. If you've ever had a bad cough, you were most likely advised to take cough suppressant. Likewise, a runny nose is medicated with cold or flu medicine, which suppresses the mucous. After a day or so, we tend to misdiagnose our condition, thinking that, because the symptoms are no longer visible, the sickness is gone. However, it is simply lying dormant within the body. So, many of us unwittingly continue to walk around with infectious diseases, which cause more serious health concerns down the road. On the other hand, vomiting has a way of removing sickness that lies within the body. Even though it is a gagging, violent, and uncomfortable experience, it forces everything out. Interestingly, after such a painful experience, we often feel better and our health is restored.

Emotions work similarly. When we suppress our emotions, they tend to manifests in other unhealthy ways, often leading to anger, isolation, violence, emotional shutdowns, and other toxic behaviors that place the marriage and family in a vulnerable state. When we fully acknowledge our emotions and express them, we are allowed to properly handle life's situations and resolve conflict.

The next unproductive response is that of the winner. The winner typically responds in one of two ways. The first is to ignore his spouse's perspective, taking things into his own hands. This is known as *independent behavior*, which is when someone makes plans and decisions that go against his partner's will, without consideration for the other person's perspective. Independent behavior is a problem in marriage because we often have a tendency to do what makes us happy, even when it makes our spouse unhappy, creating a win-lose scenario. We don't feel the pain our spouse feels when we are inconsiderate. All we feel is the pleasure we gain. Independent behavior creates a mountain of resentment and mistrust in a marriage, keeping conflict alive.

The second possible response of the winner is to stubbornly hold to her position as long as humanly possible, until the loser breaks. This can be done through persuasion, manipulation, and guilt. While the winner gets what she wants, the loser grudgingly goes along to get along.

In both scenarios there is a clear winner and a clear loser. Each individual within the partnership has a very different philosophy and relational code of ethics by which they govern their individual lives. The loser often looks at making sacrifices for her spouse as the golden standard of marital love. Meanwhile, the winner has an, 'I know what's best, so things should be done my way,' mentality. These conflicting philosophies initially accommodate one another. Unfortunately, over time, this win-lose pattern creates inequality within the relationship. Then, something unexpected happens. The loser goes rogue, eventually becoming fed up and refusing to continually accommodate her spouse with no clear reciprocation. She's sick and tired of losing all the time. She now either wants change, or wants out of the relationship. The loser is now convinced that her partner doesn't care as much about her, leading to feelings of resentment. Meanwhile, the winner is wondering why the loser would ever want to interrupt a system that has been working for so many years. All along he thought everything was fine. The news of this discontent rocks his world. As the loser finds her voice and begins to speak up, the couple quickly winds up in crisis if the information isn't well received.

In order to overcome conflict in your marriage, you must engage in perfect harmony. Perfect harmony should always be the goal for making decisions within a marriage. In perfect harmony, you strive for a win-win outcome, which is the opposite of compromise.

Successful Marital Negotiation

Conflict resolution is by far one of the most important skills needed for any successful relationship. Much different from compromise, conflict resolution creates a win-win scenario for both parties. In fact, if you review the definitions of *compromise* and *negotiate*, you can see similarities between the two. However, they are different in their application.

Compromise means to adjust or settle by mutual concession; to come to an agreement by mutual concession; or to find a way between extremes.

Negotiate means to confer with another in order to arrive at the settlement of some matter; to deal with some matter or affair that requires stability for its successful handling; or to successfully travel along or over.

A vast difference in these two concepts comes when simply applied. Most couples gravitate toward compromise. Yet our version of compromise is often plagued with having to give up a part of ourselves in order to make peace, whereas negotiation is getting something we both want.

Win-win is about making sure both parties have their needs or goals met, while creating as much mutual value as time and resources allow. Each partner is willing to invest more time and energy into finding solutions. The mantra is, "It's not enough that I win; I will not be happy until you have won too." This is the perfect attitude to have as you go through the negotiation process.

My mentor, Dr. Willard Harley, provides a simple four-step process that I take my clients through when helping to resolve issues. Initially, I discover how many issues exist. For every issue that is clearly identified, I provide the couple with a marriage negotiation worksheet for that particular issue. If there are twelve issues, they get twelve sheets. I then explain that there are four steps to the negotiation process.

Step One: Establishing Ground Rules
Create ground rules on how to effectively communicate throughout the negotiation in order to ensure its success. There are three ground rules that must be uncompromisingly adhered to.

- Ground Rule #1 - Remain Positive Throughout the Negotiation

  Couples tend to become upset and defensive when discussing how they feel or how they have been treated. It is important to prepare, individually, for the possibility of critiques and stay positive and cheerful despite what is said.

- Ground Rule #2 – Create a Safe Environment

  It is critically important to create a safe and accepting environment, free from judgment or fear of punishment. If neither person feels safe discussing sensitive matters, both will become tight-lipped.

- Ground Rule #3 – Take a Break

  Rome wasn't built in a day and neither are negotiations. It may take several hours or days to work through an issue. So, if you reach a point at which the problem doesn't seem to be going anywhere, demands are being made, or someone is being disrespectful, stop negotiating and come back to the subject later. When you are ready to return to negotiating, discuss how to avoid negativity before jumping in again.

Step Two: Identify the Problem and Investigate Each Other's Perspectives

Make sure you both have a mutual understanding of what the problem is. All too often, couples jump into negotiation with no real understanding of the issue. Each has an incomplete understanding of what the other is thinking or feeling. I know couples who have spent hours arguing back and forth, only to find out that they weren't even clear on what the issue was. Clarifying and analyzing the problem helps to resolve it much faster.

On the worksheet, first write down the issue in a clear and concise manner. Next, write down your personal perspective on the issue. Finally, wright down what you believe your spouse's perspective is.

Step Three: Brainstorm Solutions

On the worksheet, you must write down every possible solution you can think of to solve the problem. During brainstorming, quantity is better than quality. Don't restrain your mind. Instead, let it run free to think of all the possible things that could work for the both of you.

Step Four: Choose a Solution That Meets the Conditions of Perfect Harmony

Up to this point, it is recommended that you do the steps individually. The best procedure is to be one with your worksheet, writing down your answers as you see them best. Step 4 is the only step you should do together. When you are prepared to talk, it must be done in a specific way.

Take your answered worksheet and read exactly what you have written down. Do not talk about it, explain it, or adlib. This is where we get into trouble. Our communication styles often get in the way of effective dialogue. Sharp words, tonality, and body language destroy our best intentions. As each of you read steps 1-3, take the time to clarify anything that your partner may have gotten wrong in his or her write up. Once both of you have read your ideas, it's time to negotiate in perfect harmony.

To be in harmony with your spouse means to be in agreement. Interestingly, the Greek word for *agree* is the word *sumphoneo*, from where we get the word symphony. Agreement among instruments ensures a musical symphony without discord. When couples mutually and enthusiastically agree without discord, they are in perfect harmony with one another. So, review each other's list of possible solutions. Circle the solutions you both enthusiastically agree with. Then make a decision to implement those solutions immediately. Spend a few days implementing each possible solution until you find one that works. Once you've found the sweet spot, celebrate your victory. A conflict that you've struggled with for months, possibly years, is now resolved!

I know it sounds unrealistic to get such big results in so little time. That's exactly what my clients thought before they truly embraced the process and utilized the tool. People ask me, "Does this thing really work?" My response is always, "It will work if you work it." It's just that simple.

From Power Struggle to Power Couple

As mentioned in previous chapters, marriage is God's secret weapon for His kingdom's domination of the earth. However, when couples are in compromise, conflict, or crisis, they cannot be used as a divine vessel for God's glory. Satan knows this. He does all he can to keep us divided, consistently stirring things up within the home. He knows that a house divided against itself cannot stand.

There are three accounts in the Gospels in which Jesus states that a kingdom divided against itself is laid waste, or a house divided cannot stand: Luke 11:17, Mark 3:25, and Matthew 12:25. Jesus's logical argument to the Pharisees was that a kingdom at cross-purposes with itself will fall. Likewise, any household driven by infighting will tear itself apart. By saying that a house divided cannot stand, Jesus illustrates the fact that success relies on congruency. Psalm 133:1 says, "How good and pleasant it is when God's people live together in unity!" This does not apply only to the church, but to marriage as well. Agreement is essential for marital success. When couples choose to govern their lives upon the principles of agreement and perfect harmony, they remove all power struggles, placing themselves on the path of a power couple.

One of the things that makes a power couple so powerful is the unity between them. When two come together on one accord, nothing can stop them. There is an indelible force that brings about results more rapidly and with less effort. They tap into the power of the marriage mastermind, which is a coordination of knowledge and effort, in a spirit of harmony between a husband and wife, for the attainment of a definite purpose. When two minds merge, they create an invisible, intangible, force that is likened to a third mind. Mastermind groups share the basic philosophy that more can be accomplished in less time by working together. Margaret Mead said, "Never doubt that a small group of thoughtful, committed citizens can change the world. Indeed, it is the only thing that ever has." When this concept is properly understood, couples no longer compete with one another; instead, they find reasons to cooperate.

James Surowiecki, in his book *The Wisdom of Crowds*, points out that a group has a larger intelligence than an individual. As individuals, we have the ability to see things from our own perspective, our own worldview. By adding others to the mix, the group has a greater ability to share a combined intellect, seeing things from a new and different perspective. This is what some call the third mind. It is this collective third mind that processes information down to its core essence. It is there that thoughts crystallize into ideas. It is also there that the "Aha!" moment occurs. As individuals, we cannot achieve this because our short-sighted views cloud our perspectives. As a collaborative unit, with a more objective view of the world, the possibilities for expansive thinking and manifestation are endless.

Author Napoleon Hill spent his entire career interviewing business titans and teaching success laws to the masses. He is one of the first individuals to introduce the mastermind concept to the public. He believed that, "The blending of the minds of men and women produced the most effective alliances of them all." In other words, no matter how successful men and women may be when aligned with others in their own gender group, it pales in comparison to the unity of the male/female mind.

Furthermore, an enormous amount of published research on the brain has revealed the dramatic anatomical, chemical, hormonal, and psychological differences between the male and female brain. These differences are known to impact emotions, thinking, and behavior. According to Louann Brizendine, MD, a neuropsychiatrist at the University of California in San Francisco, "There is no unisex brain. Girls arrive already wired as girls, and boys arrive already wired as boys. Their brains are different by the time they're born." It is these very differences that create perfect harmony once united. What's most exciting about this information is that there is medical research proving that there is a major benefit in the joining of the male and female minds!

Napoleon Hill went on to say, "A man and wife may live

together, accumulate a fair sized (or greater) fortune, and rear and educate a family without the bond of harmony, which is essential for the development of a Master Mind. But all of these alliances might be made more powerful and effective if based upon a foundation of perfect harmony, thus permitting the development of a supplemental power known as the Master Mind." If this concept of a mastermind, and the power of unity sounds foreign to you, let's take a peek inside the Word and see what the scripture reveals.

The bible talks about the power of agreement in a multitude of ways. First, according to Matthew 18:20, Jesus said, "For where two or three are gathered together in my name, there am I in the midst of them." In other words, when two or more believers operate according to their Kingdom rights, coordinating in a spirit of perfect harmony, and working toward a definite objective, they place themselves in a position to access the supernatural realm.

Second, when we are in conflict with one another, our prayers won't work. 1 Peter 3:7 says, "In the same way, you husbands must give honor to your wives. Treat your wife with understanding as you live together... Treat her as you should so your prayers will not be hindered." So, perfect harmony and prayer in marriage are essential to activating the supernatural. Just as the prayer of agreement between two or more is a multiplication of the prayer of faith, the powers that the prayer of faith releases is amplified many times when two or more people pray it together. The prayer of agreement unleashes tremendous power that shakes even the heavens. In the Old Testament, in Deuteronomy 32:30, we read that one of the Covenant people could put a thousand to flight, and two could put ten thousand to flight. So, when two or more Christians get into agreement, there is a tremendous amplification of spiritual power.

Third, on the negative side of things, the Tower of Babel is a perfect example of the power of agreement. This story in Genesis 11:6 reveals the unlimited potential of unified men. Even though their desire to build a temple to the heavens to bring glory to themselves was supernaturally thwarted, God said that nothing that they proposed would be withheld from them. For good or for evil, there is no doubt that two heads are better than one. So, even when evil men conspire to do wickedness in the land, unless God intervenes, they can access the same power that the believer can because agreement is a law, and there is power within the law. If you obey the law, the law will obey you. Furthermore, when we are in agreement with God and His will, our plans are sure to succeed.

Lastly, Jesus said to His disciples in Matthew 18:19, "Truly I tell you that if two of you on earth agree about anything they ask for, it will be done for them by my Father in heaven. This is a conditional promise that requires only two things: (1) that the disciples be on earth and (2) that they be in agreement. So, when we pay attention to what God is saying about the power of agreement, we should get excited. If these promises are made for both the sinner and the saint, how less true could it be for two individuals who function within a three-fold covenant relationship with God?

God has big plans for covenant partners. Their level of power and influence on the earth is unlimited. There are only two obstacles preventing couples from manifesting God's glory in the earth. The first is the devil, who tries his best to keep couples in conflict. The second is couples themselves, for refusing to believe that there is a divine assignment and supernatural ability that has been given to them. When we begin to truly understand our purpose for marriage, we must create a biblical mantra that says, "Nothing will be restrained from us...Anything we ask shall be done for us." We need to say it every day, several times a day, until we embody it. When we truly embrace this truth, every husband and wife will strive to do everything possible to stay out of conflict.

Additional Conflict Resolution Techniques

1. Sincerely commit to making the Bible the final authority in your lives and marriage. This is a decision to embrace your relationship with God, not religion. Jesus told His disciples in John 14:15, "If ye love me, keep my commandments." Likewise, as believers, we must find practical solutions and guidelines for marriage and family life within the Word of God. When we submit to God's biblical standards, the spousal tug-of-war is eradicated.

2. Give up the need to be right. If either one of you are committed to being right, then your spouse will always be wrong by default. However, when you give up your need to be right, you become more teachable and the probability of resolution significantly increases.

3. Never threaten your spouse with divorce. People carelessly throw that word around, usually with no intention of acting on such a threat. Rather, it is used to control and manipulate a person or situation. Instead, make a verbal pledge to life-long commitment, making you both feel secure during times of emotional vulnerability.

4. Listen beyond your spouse's words and tonality. Instead, listen to each other's hearts, even if you disagree with the appropriateness of those feelings.

5. Stay out of the shadows of the past. Limit conflicts to the here and now. Never bring up past failures, since all previous failures should be resolved and forgiven. If they aren't, find another time to address those separately.

6. Absolutely stay away from absolutes. Phrases such as "You never" or "You always" should be eliminated from your vocabulary. These are exaggerated phrases are probably not well received by your spouse, especially if you are looking for genuine resolution.

7. Find marriage mentors. When you reach roadblocks, rather than agreeing to disagree, find another couple to represent wisdom in the areas with which you struggle. Mutually submit to their wisdom to help correct issues in your marriage.

8. Even though your spouse won't always be correct, consider your mate an instrument of God working in your life. Proverbs 12:1 says, "He who hates reproof is stupid."

9. Remember that the resolution of the conflict is what is important- not who wins or loses. If the conflict is resolved, you both win. You're on the same team, not opposing ones.

10. Pray about each conflict before discussing it with your spouse. Furthermore, pray with your spouse before discussing a sensitive issue. The presence of God will create a calmer atmosphere, allowing you to deal with.

Couples Testimonial from
Demond & Jasmin Mason
Atlanta, Georgia

WOW!!! What an awesome weekend my wife and I experienced at the Couples Academy Retreat! We learned so many valuable tools to help FIREPROOF our marriage and become the power couple that God ordained for us to be! Hasani and Danielle powerfully taught great principles and gave us tools and assignments that caused us to reconnect with each other and communicate in healthy ways. The activities helped reveal to us the strengths and areas of opportunity in our marriage and worked hand in hand with the lessons.We are looking forward to the future couples retreat with Couples Academy! Thanks again for a wonderful, life and marriage-transforming weekend.

chapter four

Dwell with Your
S P O U S E
According to Knowledge

Boy meets Girl. Boy says, "Hi, my name is John. Will you marry me?" Girl says, "Sure!"

I know this may sound ridiculous, but many relationships operate this way. I have met several couples who fell in love and quickly ran to the altar in search of marital bliss. Each set of circumstances are different, but the result is ultimately the same: two people got married too soon, knowing too little about each other, and now they feel like they are in too deep. Do all of these marriages fail? Absolutely not! My aunt married her husband six months after meeting him and they've been married for over 45 years.

While many share a similar experience to my aunt's, others have a very different story to tell. I know one couple who quickly wed before the husband's induction into the military. Another couple, both of a certain age, got married because they believed courting was a waste of time. Yet, another couple ran down the aisle to avoid the temptation of sex, believing that it was better to marry than to burn.

Then, there are many couples who have had lengthy courtships, yet still haven't taken the time to truly discover one another. So many things contribute to this scenario, but two stand out: pre-marital sex and co-habitation. When sex is introduced into a relationship too soon, it becomes the focus, shifting most of the communication and interaction in that direction. More time is spent on sexual exploration than on mutual personal discovery. Likewise, when couples cohabitate, it thrusts their relationship into hyper speed. Engaging in sex and dealing with household and family affairs significantly matures a relationship, even if it is only months old. As a result, couples spend no real time discovering each other.

Does this mean that couples should be together for a pre-determined amount of time before they are qualified to wed? Not necessarily. There is no magic number of months or years that will ensure marital success. However, I do believe that there are specific seasons a relationship should experience. Ecclesiastes 3:1 says, "To everything there is a season and a time to every purpose under the heaven."

This means that when God created the heavens and the earth, He established order. The seasons of earth are spring, summer, autumn, and winter- each lasting about three months, bringing changes in temperature, weather, and the length of the days. Genesis 8:22 says, "While the earth remaineth, seedtime and harvest, and cold and heat, and summer and winter, and day and night shall not cease."

So, the seasons are permanent periods of time that have a profound effect on the behaviors of people. For instance, if it's summertime and you go outside dressed in a corduroy sweat suit, you will burn up. Likewise, if it's winter and you go outside dressed in a t-shirt and shorts, you will freeze to death. Each season is comprised of extremely different variations that determine what is appropriate. Just as the earth has four seasons, so do relationships. They are: dating, committed courtship, engagement, and marriage. In order to move on to the next season, you must properly function within your current season, each of which calls for differences in level of commitment, rules, conduct, and responsibility.

Sadly, many couples jump from one season to the next, sometimes even skipping over seasons, in order to get to the wedding. This behavior presents a major problem- skipping seasons in relationships is like picking fruit too soon. Fruit picked from a vine prematurely is robbed of the vital nutrients normally obtained during the growth and development process. Therefore, if it is eaten before it is fully ripe, it will taste bitter. Similarly, if it is picked and eaten too late, the fruit will turn rotten and spoil. However, when properly ripened, one can truly enjoy the sweet nectar of the fruit. So, fruit must be picked and eaten at the appropriate time in order for it to produce a positive result. The concept is the same for relationships. A relationship must progress through each of the four seasons at the right time in order to produce a positive result.

While there is no required amount of time for a couple to date before entering into a deeper level of commitment, embracing the four seasons is essential for your success. According to Thomas Stanley's *Millionaire Mindset,* ninety percent of a person's failures or successes are determined by their selection of a mate. Therefore, I would highly recommend that couples be together no less than a year before determining if marriage is the right option.

Become A Student of Your Spouse

I have always been a student at heart. I love to learn, search, and research. I get excited every time I gain new insight on a topic of interest. I read a new book every two weeks and spend lots of time watching documentaries. My favorite subjects are history, politics, philosophy, religion, science, psychology, and economics. However, it is not my education that qualifies me to dwell in a happy home. My degree, certifications, book collection, and intellectual storehouse don't put a smile on my wife's face. They don't win her heart. All the knowledge in the world won't secure my marriage because a happy and fulfilling marriage requires a completely different knowledge base and set of skills. 1 Peter 3:7 says, "Likewise, ye husbands, dwell with them according to knowledge, giving honor unto the wife, as unto the weaker vessel, and as being heirs together of the grace of life; that your prayers be not hindered."

While this scripture pertains to how a husband should deal with his wife, it is a principle that can also work in reverse. It is equally important for wives to dwell with their husbands according to knowledge. Unfortunately, most of us have over emphasized love as being the key ingredient for marital success. While it is important, the success of a marriage is not guaranteed by love. Love brings happiness, but it does not make a marriage work. The only things that make anything work are knowledge and skill. For instance, you may love your car, but it will eventually break down if you do not dwell with it according to knowledge.

I once met a woman who was the proud owner of a brand new Mercedes Benz. She loved her car. She took pictures with it, spoke highly of it, and spent quality time driving it. She was emotionally invested in her vehicle, but within a few months things started to change. It didn't ride as smoothly as it once did, lights began appearing in the dashboard, and it would occasionally overheat. The car eventually died before reaching the first year anniversary.

When things were going well, this woman believed that God had answered her prayers by blessing her with the car of her dreams. However, when things started going wrong, she began to question God's will, the salesman's integrity, and the car's capability. Ultimately, she questioned whether or not she'd made the right decision. Once the car died she was devastated, but rather than do the necessary work to repair the vehicle, she divorced her Mercedes Benz by trading it in for a brand new Jaguar. Unfortunately, the same thing will happen with her Jaguar in about one year's time and it won't be God's fault, the salesman's fault, nor the car's fault. It will be her fault.

Why? She will continue to do what she's always done-remain ignorant about her car by failing to read the manual and gain the knowledge and skill necessary to care for it. She will fail to realize that she needs to change the oil, rotate the tires, replace the brake pads, maintain the fluids, and schedule routine check-ups. She will continue to do nothing more than put gas in the tank, eventually driving her brand new car into the ground. As strange as this may sound, we do the same exact thing with our marriages by believing that love conquers all. If that were true, the bible would not say that husbands need to dwell with their wives according to knowledge.

One of the core principles that we teach at Couples Academy is that every individual should become a student of their partner. Generally, when people talk about being a student, it is in the context of formal education. In fact, the average person can spend anywhere from twelve to twenty years entrenched in education. The last thing most people want to hear is that they must become a student again. However, the same focus, intensity, and time commitment that people put into their schooling, careers, and personal passions is required for marriage as well. Some of you are reading this thinking, *It shouldn't take all of that, I didn't sign up for this,* or *Why does this have to be so hard?*

Well, suppose someone offered you a tremendous sum of money, but the exact amount would be determined by how well you could learn to speak French over the next two months. You would embark on the most intense, crash-course program of learning in your life! You would study from morning to night. You would be burning the midnight oil, listening to language tapes, carrying flash cards wherever you went, and seeking out fluent French speakers to practice with. During those two months, no one could drag you near a time-wasting television program. You would allow nothing other than necessary, life sustaining physical activities to interfere. You would do all of this for money. It's amazing how many people can justify sacrificing marriage, family, food, and sleep to pursue their deepest desires, yet they will not make any legitimate sacrifices to ensure the successes of their marriages. They assume that they know all they need to know about their spouse. That way of thinking is not only erroneous- it is dangerous.

There's an awesome concept called *Moon-to-Earth Syndrome*. If you look up into the sky at night, you will see a bright moon. However, you see only one side of it. If you want to see the other side of the moon, you would have to travel into space to get a different angle. The unseen side is referred to as the 'dark side of the moon'. Much like the moon, each of us has a dark side. The word 'dark' doesn't necessarily imply evil, sinister, or wicked. In this case, it represents our undiscovered side, implying that there are things about our partners that we haven't yet discovered. Much like the moon has many faces (half- moon, crescent moon, full moon, etc.), we also have many faces. We are sophisticated beings with many interests, passions, and desires. Therefore, we must take time and be intentional in discovering those within each other.

Let The Lessons Begin

Education shouldn't be reserved for a classroom alone. Learning should be a continuous process that you embrace throughout the course of your life. When you embrace the concept of always being a student, life becomes your classroom. In order to be a successful student, you must understand one important concept: *In school, the student is given the lesson and then expected to pass to the test.* In life, the student is given the test and then expected to learn the lesson. If you don't learn the lessons that life brings you, you will continue to face the same tests again and again until you pass. The sad reality is that many couples aren't good learners, so they continue to fail the same tests for years. If failure is inevitable, why not fail new tests rather than the same old ones.

There is often so much hurt, disappointment, and mistrust in marriages that spouses have a hard time interchangeably playing the teacher-student role with one another, but it is important to allow your spouse to be your teacher. Unfortunately, many people suffer from the "I Already Know That" syndrome, which is a dangerous thing because knowing something and doing what you know are two very different things.

In order for couples to truly excel, they must be teachable. There are two variables to assist you in finding out just how teachable you are. The first is willingness to learn-On a scale of 1 to 10, what is your willingness to learn? The second variable is willingness to accept change- On a scale of 1 to 10, how willing are you to accept change. On both scales, one represents low willingness, while ten represents high willingness. Be honest when choosing your numbers.

What are your scores? Are you highly teachable? Interestingly, this is the very first concept that I share with couples when we begin our journey together. I hear all types responses from spouses that come into my office, the numbers ranging from one end of the spectrum to the other. Sometimes it is revealed that a person is highly teachable in one area, but unteachable in the other. The key to marital success is to be highly teachable in both areas- willingness to learn and willingness to accept change. Proverbs 24:3-4 tells us that a successful marriage and family life are directly related to knowledge and the willingness to act upon it. It says, "By wisdom a house is built, and by understanding it is established; by knowledge the rooms are filled with all precious and pleasant riches."

With that understanding, let the lessons begin.

Lesson#1: Get Your School Supplies

Back-to-school preparation remains a top priority every year as the summer wanes. With four children to prepare, weeks are spent buying new clothes, getting school supplies, visiting classrooms, and talking to teachers. It is an arduous task that must be done each and every year to ensure their success in a new learning environment. Luckily, the preparation needed for spouses isn't nearly as in-depth. There are three supplies that I highly recommend every couple obtain.

First, get a quality leather-bound journal and name it, "The Book of _____", putting your spouse's name in the blank space. For example, my journal is named, "The Book of Danielle." Most couples live life on auto-pilot and don't pay attention to the details of life. I suggest recording those details. As you experience life together and learn more about each other, you should write down your partner's likes and dislikes. Notate the things that turn your partner on and off. Record your partner's attitude, moods, and temperament. Note the things that trigger changes. Write down their emotional reactions, important discussions, and every day habits and routines. Treat your partner like a subject, studying everything you can about him or her. The more you observe and record, the more successful you will be in dealing with your partner on a day-to-day basis.

Next, get a two-pocket folder to store all paperwork and documents you accumulate throughout your journey together. It is so easy to misplace important documentation when there is no official home for it. When you become a Couples Academy client you receive a set of two folders for storing materials.

Finally, take advantage of your smart phone. Personally, my iPhone is my best friend. Whenever Danielle and I have an important conversation, one worthy of my undivided attention, I grab my phone and open up my recording app. No matter how attentive you may be, the average person only remembers ten percent of what is communicated. Typically, that ten percent is what is heard last. A recorded call acts as a third-party witness that can help resolve misunderstandings. Just as you may record an important lecture given by a professor, record important conversations with your spouse to review later.

Lesson #2: Unlearn All That You've Learned

In *Star Wars: The Empire Strikes Back*, Yoda gives Luke Skywalker some advice. He tells Luke, "You must unlearn what you have learned." What he means is that, in order for Luke to operate at his full potential, he must disregard all of his limiting beliefs. Along the way, we all accumulate beliefs that do not serve us or our relationships. Release them. Many of our convictions and deeply imbedded beliefs are based upon erroneous notions.

There are countless women imprisoning their husbands with their own interpretation of manhood, which does not line up with who their husbands are. They look at their husbands through the filter of their fathers, brothers, male friends, or former lovers. An unfair comparison is made that these men often cannot live up to. Maybe he doesn't make enough, isn't handy enough, isn't smart enough, isn't romantic enough, or doesn't do enough. As a result, he can never be enough. Her constant reminders of these perceived shortcomings make him feel emasculated, inferior, inadequate, and incompetent.

Likewise, husbands can hold their wives to very high standards and unrealistic expectations which can feel deflating to her. Her worth is measured by physical attractiveness, sexual performance and availability, cooking and cleaning capability, parenting skills, and her ability to contribute to the financial security of the home. If she falls below his level of expectation in any of these areas, her womanhood is brought into question.

Whether we gather our beliefs regarding gender from society, the media, or our own personal experiences, we must look at our spouses from a healthy perspective. While it is good to have a basis of knowledge of the duties of a husband and wife, we must also take the time to discover individual uniqueness. Husbands and wives should always be on a quest for inner growth and self-development, never settling for their own personal weaknesses and shortcomings. At the same time, we should explore and embrace the unique expressions of our spouse's individuality, while not condemning them to a template that doesn't fit.

Therefore, we must unlearn what we have learned and learn something new. Unlearning can be described as stripping the existing paint from a wall so that new paint sticks. As you may know, stripping is the biggest part of the job. Unlearning means letting go of what we have already learned or acquired. It is not about right or wrong. It is about being open to and exploring something that lies beneath judgment- right and wrong. When you decide to unlearn something, you open yourself up to a world of opportunities with your spouse.

Lesson #3: Study Your Spouse

The following is a comprehensive list of free resources that you and your partner can use to gain a tremendous amount of knowledge about each other. These quizzes and questionnaires will help you to properly love, communicate, and meet each other's sexual, emotional, and financial needs. Please download all of the suggested documents, complete them, and share your answers with your spouse. Use your partner's completed documents as cheat sheets on how to treat him or her.

1. Pillow Talk: 50 Questions for Extraordinary Sex-
http://couplesacademy.org/
2. Intellectual Intimacy: Questions for Couples-
http://couplesacademy.org/
3. The Five Love Languages Test and Challenge-
http://www.5lovelanguages.com/
4. Emotional Needs Questionnaire-
http://www.marriagebuilders.com/
5. Love Busters Questionnaire-
http://www.marriagebuilders.com/
6. Personal History Questionnaire-
http://www.marriagebuilders.com/
7. Marriage Negotiation Worksheet-
http://www.marriagebuilders.com/
8. Monthly Cashflow Plan-
https://www.daveramsey.com/budgeting/how-to-budget/

These tools will allow you and your partner to enjoy a deeper level of intimacy. Most of us have had the experience of discovering something new about our spouse and saying, "You never told me that!", only to hear the reply, "You never asked." Information may not have been concealed from us, but our spouse may have thought the information was not important or worth sharing until the topic came up. These resources provide a platform for two individuals to get to know one another in a more meaningful and structured way.

Intimacy requires transparency. It is a word that has often been described with the homonymous phrase 'Into-Me-See.' It requires allowing a person inside your heart and mind. By learning all you can about your partner, discussing issues before they become problems, revealing unexpressed agreements and assumptions, and looking deeply at what matters to you, your chances of dwelling successfully with your partner will greatly increase.

Lesson #4: The Teacher Must Become a Student Again
Peter Drucker said, "We now accept the fact that learning is a lifelong process of keeping abreast of change. And the most pressing task is to teach people how to learn." The point here is that you should never stop learning because life never stops teaching. Whether you are degreed, accredited, or self-taught, your level of education should humble you, not make you pompous. Why? The more you learn the more you realize how much you do not know.

It is important to look at marriage as a continuous learning process. I find it interesting that couples spend upwards of twelve months preparing for their wedding day and approximately four hours in pre-marital classes. Not only do they go into the marriage knowing very little, even less time is spent educating themselves afterwards. The overwhelming majority of couples who come into my office know very little about the inner workings of their spouse and just as little about relationship dynamics in general. So, when I am asked to give my professional opinion on whether they should consider divorce as an option, I respond with a slew of questions.

Have you read a marriage book in the last six months?
Have you attended a marriage enrichment class?
Have you signed up for a couple's retreat?
Have you attended a marriage conference?
Have you sought out a marriage counselor?

The answers to these questions are generally the same- "No". So, the road to marital recovery begins with becoming students again. The most important concept that must be learned, thoroughly understood, and mastered is the difference between a marriage and a relationship. These words have been used interchangeably, but there is a major difference between the two. Each is important and each requires a different set of skils.

After working with countless clients, I have created a system that places each couple in one of four distinct quadrants:

Quadrant A: good relationship, bad marriage
Quadrant B: bad relationship, bad marriage
Quadrant C: bad relationship, good marriage
Quadrant D: good relationship, good marriage.

Relationships represent a couple's emotional fulfillment, effective communication, sexual intimacy, recreational companionship, and spiritual connection. These areas combined represent the heart-beat of any good union. Marriage, on the other hand, is the legal institution that envelops the relationship. It is known as the business-side of the relationship, representing household management, financial stewardship, delegation of roles and responsibilities, parenting, and family planning. In essence, the relationship represents the heart- emotions- and the marriage represents the head- logic and reason. It should be clear that each of these areas requires a unique set of skills that must be learned and properly developed. Neither a husband nor a wife enters into a marriage with full knowledge of the required skills.

I'm quite sure you have met couples who are in love with each other and have great chemistry, but their kids aren't disciplined and their finances are a wreck. You may also know couples who have a picture perfect marriage on paper- they live in the best neighborhoods, their kids go to the best schools, and their household runs like a well-oiled machine. However, they are emotionally disconnected, sexually frigid, and they struggle with communication.

Over time, a couple that struggles in one area will struggle in the other as well. So, certain skills are required for each area. Effective listening, true forgiveness, open and honest communication, and sexual chemistry are soft skills that are developed over time. Securing employment, cooking, cleaning, parenting, household maintenance, and budgeting are examples of hard-skills, which are non-gender specific. For a marriage to be successful, it is important for both partners to have soft and hard skills. Life together can be wonderful when husbands and wives make a decision to remain teachable- willing and able. When personal growth and self-development are the foundational principles in a marriage, everyone wins.

Couples Testimonial from
Ira & Janell Smith
Los Angeles, California

We believe everyone knows when their relationship is in need of a reinvention; however finding the courage to get help is what's difficult. we feel so blessed to have had the courage to let someone from the outside inside of our world. God's favor is what brought Hasani into our marriage and it has been forever changed. In the past together we have overcome our issues which seemed great at the time but those same issues would reoccur. With Hasani we have conquered our issues. Couples Academy is single handedly responsible for changing how we approach, receive and respect ourselves as individuals and as a couple. We are forever grateful for the program.

Place Your Marriage On The Path To Fulfillment
With CouplesAcademy.org

chapter five

Infidelity: When
GOOD PEOPLE
Do Bad Things

ONE WEEK! One week is what John had before finding out if he was HIV positive. He faced this terrifying situation through no fault of his own. It was his spouse who had broken their covenant. For months she had denied it, but was forced to admit her wrongdoing when she came home from the emergency room with a hospital wristband and penicillin. In a very nonchalant and cold way, she stood in the kitchen doorway and said, "You better go to the hospital and get yourself checked out. I just got treated for an STD."

He stood there in shock and disbelief and within ten seconds of hearing the horrifying news, he murdered her...in his mind. He had played it out over and over again. Fortunately, before reacting, he jumped in his car wearing a white tee and pajama pants (no shoes, no wallet, no cell phone), and drove and drove and drove through the night. His journey had begun in Atlanta, but before he realized it, he found himself three and a half hours away in Savannah. Now, as he replays the offense in his head he's confused. He's hurt. He's angry. He's tired. He's got one week before he finds out his fate, and two weeks before he and his children leave.

The discovery of the affair had sent his marriage into a tailspin. The days following the revelation were hell on earth, full of resentment and acts of rage. Regret and chaos consumed their depleted relationship. The thin battle line between love and hate had been laid, weapons had been drawn, and an all-out war was waged. Shattered glass, broken appliances, tattered clothing, and verbal venom became the least of their concerns. Linda's justifications for the affair were like daggers piercing his ego. Verbally paralyzed by her vicious attacks, John had stood in front of his wife boiling with rage. The left side of his upper lip twitching with disgust. His eyes turned red with the blood of revenge as beads of sweat fell from his face. "It's over!", he'd shouted. "The marriage is over!"

What happened? Is it possible that Linda forgot her Bible study lesson "thou shalt not covet thy neighbor's house" found in Exodus 20:17. Or were her actions a deliberate act of sexual self-gratification despite the consequences? No matter how you answer these questions, the vow of fidelity was no longer honored.

Unfortunately, scenarios like this are all too common. Every week my phone and email are flooded with messages from couples pleading for help. Their vows have been broken and their marriages are in a state of crisis. For most of them, Couples Academy represents their last attempt to restore their marriage. With so many marriages in need of repair, Danielle and I created *Last Chance Weekends*. It is a four day, group marriage intensive experience in which we work with a small group of five couples at a time. Much like the VH-1 reality show *Couples Therapy*, these weekends are designed to dig deep, find healing, and help restore fragmented marriages.

The couples we work with are as diverse as their marital situations. Whether they have been having multiple one-night stands, sleeping with prostitutes, engaging in emotional affairs, swinging in open marriages, experiencing severe sexual compulsion, having incestuous relationships, suffering from porn addiction, or have had a one-time violation, these couples are looking for a way to rebuild.

Along with the alarming nationwide rate of infidelity, comes a high level of ambiguity regarding betrayal. As a society we tend to underestimate, overcomplicate, or completely ignore the nature, causes, and marital patterns associated with emotional and sexual affairs. For this reason, people continue to be ensnared by very obvious pitfalls that severely impact their marriages.

Ever since Clinton's famous, "I did not have sexual relations with that woman." statement, I have noticed numerous articles and books debating on what actually constitutes an affair. Is it only classified an affair if a spouse has intercourse with a person outside of the marriage? Does oral sex count? How about fondling? Kissing? Holding hands? What about emotional affairs? Do one-night stands count as affairs, or is it only an affair when the heart is involved?

Infidelity is defined as unfaithfulness, betrayal, or lack of loyalty to a spouse or partner. Unfortunately, many people believe that, as long as a relationship is not physically consummated, it isn't considered infidelity. This belief is totally false. The slippery slope of infidelity begins long before clear violations are broken. As I've always said, 'Infidelity doesn't start in the bedroom, it ends in the bedroom.'

As an Infidelity Recovery Specialist, I have worked with couples who have presented a multitude of scenarios that appear to be different. When you strip them all down to their core, however, there are four basic classifications of affairs that must be properly examined: 1) The One-Night Stand, 2) Emotional Entanglement, 3) Sexual Compulsion, and 4) Add-On Affair. Each affair type is quite different, each with a unique set of circumstances surrounding it. With that said, it is very important to understand that a couple's affair type may consist of a combination of the four classifications. Additionally, I have worked with couples who have experienced all four affair types at different points in the marriage.

One-Night Stands

This affair type is considered to be an opportunistic experience that fulfills a lustful urge or desire. Typically, there is no real relationship between the two consenting parties. They are either strangers to one another, or they are casual acquaintances. Business trips, vacations, and social outings are breeding grounds for one-night stands. However, the more familiarity and access two individuals have, the more frequent their interactions may be. This is known as a serial one-night stand.

Emotional Entanglement

Arguably, emotional affairs are more devastating than short-lived sexual affairs. These types of inappropriate interactions involve intense emotions and matters of the heart. These are real relationships that exist parallel to a marriage. While some last for several months, others match- and sometimes exceed- the length of a marriage. In most cases, though not all, emotional entanglements involve sex. The combination of emotional and sexual intimacy creates a bond that is very difficult to break on one's own. The process of ending this type of affair requires long-term counseling because the potential for relapses can occur.

Sexual Compulsion

Marriages have been destroyed due to an inability to control an untamed sexual appetite. Spouses have allowed their flesh to steer them into a life of compulsive masturbation- with or without pornography- and multiple extramarital affairs- either online or in person. Often, one partner will engage in the constant use of pornography, unsafe sex, multiple sex partners, phone sex, cyber-sex, sexting, anonymous sex, multiple one-night stands, sexual massage, and prostitution. Unfortunately, these sexual activities have sabotaged marriages, careers, self-esteem, and life itself. Individual therapy is needed in addition to couples counseling.

Add-On Affair

This affair type is the most common existing in marriage; it is closely associated with emotional entanglement. Often, this type of affair happens when couples begin to drift apart into their own separate worlds. They no longer spend quality time together. There are no shared interests, activities, or goals. They have moved from being soulmates, to role-mates, to roommates. The lack of shared interests and activities creates a marital void, which is then fulfilled by someone outside of the marriage. A deep friendship is developed based upon a shared activity. Though this relationship does not include dating, dinners out, phone calls, or other activities outside the shared interest, spontaneous sexual activity sometimes results.

If you believe that society has gotten worse, that we've lost the values we once had, think again. Infidelity goes all the way back to biblical days, which is proof that human nature hasn't changed much. We tend to think that society gets worse with each new generation, but the same sexual scandals that exist today began thousands of years ago. Remember, there is nothing new under the sun. Let's take a closer look at biblical accounts of the four classifications of infidelity.

The One-Night Stand: David & Bathsheba

"And it came to pass in an evening tide, that David arose from his bed, and walked upon the roof of the king's house: and from the roof he saw a woman washing herself; and the woman was very beautiful to look upon." 2 Samuel 11:2

King David, heir to the throne of Israel, arose from his bed one evening to bathe in the glory of his kingdom. While strolling along the rooftop of his palace, he became mesmerized by what he saw- though it was not the surrounding nations that had been conquered throughout the years of David's illustrious reign, nor was it the sacredness of the Ark of the Covenant that had been placed within the courts of Jerusalem.

What had captured David's attention and had him spellbound was the beauty of a woman bathing. The combination of her beauty, the gentle water cascading down her curvature frame, and the dancing silhouette of the evening shadows pulsating rhythmically to her every move enticed the cravings trapped within David's loins. What had begun as a cursory glance soon became a lustful fixation. David's desire to have this woman would not allow him to retire to his chambers for all night prayer. Instead, he sent for her and they indulged in a passionate exchange.

Bathsheba being the wife of Uriah, King David's most loyal soldier, meant nothing to his lustful eye. He wanted what he wanted and would stop at nothing to get it. Bathsheba knew it was wrong to commit adultery, but to refuse a king's request could mean punishment or death.

Shortly after their one-night stand, Bathsheba discovered that she was pregnant with the child of a man she barely knew. Word of the unplanned pregnancy soon got back to King David and, backed into a corner with no thought of what to do next, David chose to cover up his sin. He ordered Uriah's death by placing him on the front lines in Israel's next battle. He then married Bathsheba so no one would discover the wickedness of his ways.

Although repentance followed David's behavior, so did the consequences of his actions. The consequences were not just a curse upon *his* life, but also upon his family and the nation of Israel. Here's a quick look:

- Consequence 1: Bathsheba became pregnant.
- Consequence 2: David killed Uriah, Bathsheba's husband, in order to hide his sin.
- Consequence 3: David and Bathsheba's baby died shortly after its birth.
- Consequence 4: David's daughter, Tamar, is raped by her half-brother Amnon.

- Consequence 5: David's third son, Absalom, avenges his sister's abuse by killing Amnon.
- Consequence 6: Absalom overthrows David's rule, taking the throne as king.
- Consequence 7: Absalom humiliates David by sleeping with his wives and concubines.
- Consequence 8: Absalom is killed in battle.

As we see, David's one act resulted in four people being killed, one person being raped, a number of wives being forced into adultery, and an entire nation being overthrown. Those were some serious consequences. The sexual sin of David did not only affect him. It effected an entire generation of people. So, if you think what you do behind closed doors is no one else's business, you are wrong. The consequences of your actions can be devastating.

Emotional Entanglement: Samson & Delilah

"And he came up, and told his father and his mother, and said, I have seen a woman in Timnath of the daughters of the Philistines: now therefore get her for me to wife." Judges 14:2

Samson was a man of enormous physical strength, who was destroyed by the power of an even greater weakness. Born to deliver Israel out of the hands of the Philistines, Samson was raised as a Nazarite- a person who took a vow to be set apart for God's service. This vow, paired with his physical strength, led to many victories against the Philistines. Among his most applauded war stories are: Samson removing the gigantic gates of the city and carrying them away on his shoulders after ripping them from their hinges all by himself; Samson setting Philistine fields afire, ruining their crops; Samson slaying a thousand Philistines all by himself, using the jawbone of a donkey for a weapon, after finding it on the ground nearby; and Samson strangling a lion with his bare hands.

Unfortunately, despite his supernatural strength and unprecedented victories, Samson will always be remembered for what he might have been. Samson was to do great things, but he allowed his undisciplined eyes to be taken off of God. Instead, he fixated on forbidden women. Interestingly, the Bible's first recorded words of Samson are, "I saw a woman... Get her for me, for she looks good to me." Unfortunately, this statement became a recurring act of disobedience, ultimately leading to his demise.

No matter how strong he was, Samson couldn't conquer his weakness for the soft nature of a woman. He lacked spiritual discretion when it came to the women he wanted, becoming attracted to the opposite sex strictly on the basis of outward appearance. He was a sucker for soft skin, a beautiful face, and a feminine frame. Samson became so preoccupied with his lustful desires, he didn't realize that God had left him.

It was forbidden by God to marry, or even mingle with, Philistine women because of their worship of pagan gods. However, the lustful desire of Samson's eyes surpassed his desire to please God. Against the advice of his parents, Samson insisted on marrying a Philistine woman from Timnath. He later enjoyed the forbidden pleasures of Philistine prostitutes from Gaza. However, no woman could woo Samson like Delilah, a Philistine woman from the valley of Sorek.

Delilah was beautiful, and she knew how to wear a dress to make a brother scream. Delilah proved that even strong men harbor hidden weaknesses. Night after night he spent an incalculable number of hours with her in her home. Her charm and flawless appearance turned Samson into a hopeless romantic. Unfortunately, she was a deceitful woman with honey on her lips and poison in her heart. Pretending to love Samson, Delilah conspired with the Philistines to bring him to his knees in exchange for eleven hundred shekels of silver.

She said to Samson, "Tell me the secret of your great strength and how you can be tied up and subdued." Now, common sense should have told Samson that Delilah was up to no good, but love will make you dumb, deaf, blind, and completely out of your mind. Rather than flowing in the spirit of discernment, Samson was stuck on stupid. Delilah made three separate attempts to discover the secret to his strength. Every time, Samson misled her. However, after weeks of nagging, prodding, and whining, Samson gave in. The Bible states that Samson was "vexed by her constant nagging." Some translations say that Samson was "annoyed to death." Delilah threw herself on him, sobbing, "You hate me! You don't really love me..." So, with no hope for peace in his home, he told her everything:

"No razor has ever been used on my head because I have been a Nazarite set apart to God since birth. If my head were shaved, my strength would leave me, and I would become as weak as any other man." Judges 16:17.

106

After Samson's heartfelt confession, Delilah put him to sleep on her lap. That same night, Delilah led the Philistine soldiers to Samson. Shackled and shaven by a merciless legion of Philistine soldiers, Samson's strength became a memory of the past. They chained him to a huge stone wheel, pulling him through the city as a conquered warrior for all the nation to see. Then, they blinded him by using a hot poker to burn his eyes out of their sockets. It is interesting that the very things that got Samson into trouble were the things that were stripped from him: his eyes. His wandering eyes led to his demise. No matter how good someone may look, never allow your eyes to cause you to disobey God. Delilah's beauty caused Samson to have a love for her that he had for no other woman. He was emotionally entangled with her, which made him vulnerable to her. Despite his physical stature, Sampson was a He-Man with a She-Weakness.

Sexual Compulsion/Multiple Partners: Hosea and Gomer

"For their mother has played the harlot; she who conceived them has acted shamefully. For she said, 'I will go after my lovers, who give me my bread and my water, my wool and my flax, my oil and my drink." Hosea 2:5

Hosea was recognized as one of the greatest prophets of the eighth century B.C. Through his preaching, he taught vital truths about the love of God. According to the book of Hosea, the Lord had him marry a prostitute named Gomer. Soon after their wedding, they had a son. After that, she went on to bear two more children that he refused to claim as his

107

own because they were children of adultery, conceived in disgrace.

Hosea was faithful to his wife, but Gomer kept wandering into the arms of other lovers- again and again and again. She had little affection for her husband, believing that others had the ability to provide her more sexual gratification and material possessions than Hosea. So, she continued to indulge in the throes of passion by prostituting herself. At some point, Gomer realized she was better off with Hosea and wanted to return home, but Hosea was not prepared to take his wayward wife back. With nowhere to go and no means of provision, she sold herself into slavery. God instructed Hosea to go after her and bring her back home:

"The Lord said to me, 'Go, show your love to your wife again, though she is loved by another man and is an adulteress. Love her as the Lord loves the Israelites, though they turn to other gods and love the sacred raisin cakes.' So I bought her for fifteen shekels of silver and about a homer and a lethek of barley. Then I told her, 'You are to live with me many days; you must not be a prostitute or be intimate with any man, and I will behave the same way toward you.'"
Hosea 3:1-3

Can you imagine God telling you to rescue your spouse from a life of slavery that she voluntarily sold herself into? Nevertheless, Hosea did it despite the embarrassment that Gomer had brought to his home and family. God then instructed Hosea to show his love for her. Loving her must have been a harder task than marrying her. It's one thing to marry a prostitute, but loving her after multiple acts of infidelity must require supernatural powers and abilities.

Once she returned home, the plan was set. Hosea provided clear boundaries for their life together. Gomer would be betrothed to him for many days, during which time she wouldn't prostitute herself or be with another man. Hosea would act the same toward Gomer until she had proven her loyalty to him. Only then would their normal marital lifestyle resume. Before Hosea would emotionally reengage, he needed evidence that she had changed her lifestyle and that she was prepared to be a loyal wife.

Marital Void: Potiphar & His Wife SEP

"And it came to pass after these things, that his master's wife cast her eyes upon Joseph; and she said, Lie with me."
Genesis 39:7

Potiphar's wife, by anyone's standards, would be considered well-to-do. Potiphar was a high ranking officer to the Pharaoh of Egypt. He was a man of power, personality, and prestige. His hard work and dedication to service provided them a spacious and luxuriously furnished home, a bountiful amount of food and clothing, and an abundance of wealth. She was rendered a sizable household staff that catered to her every beck-and-call. She wanted for nothing, appearing to possess everything that any woman could ever hope for: a good man and a life of luxury. Externally, she was the object of every woman's envy.

However, there was a longing hidden deep within her heart that led her down a very dangerous path. Potiphar's wife lacked her greatest desire: Potiphar. She was neglected and rejected by the one thing that had once brought her joy. Potiphar was married to his work, thus giving his wife very little time. So, needing fulfillment and a sense of satisfaction, she found someone to occupy her time. His name was Joseph.

Joseph was commissioned by Potiphar, as his top aide, to care for his home. This young slave boy was entrusted with all that he had because Potiphar recognized that Joseph had the favor of God upon his life. However, all that Potiphar's wife chose to recognize was Joseph's sex appeal. The Bible says that Joseph was "well-built and handsome." Daily, Joseph would innocently parade his young, attractive, well-built physique self around the palace without thought of an admirer.

Engrossed with an unfulfilled yearning for attention from an absent husband, and consumed with the desire to fulfill a sexual craving, the Bible says that Potiphar's wife "cast her eyes upon Joseph and propositioned him to indulge in a sacred ritual of oneness within the confines of her marital quarters." To cast one's eyes upon something is to select or to be assigned to that particular thing. Well, wooing Joseph into a sexual relationship became her only obsession and assignment. "Come to bed with me!" was the one plea that she relentlessly insisted that Joseph fulfill. She tried to get Joseph to sexually succumb to her seductive stare. The Bible says that she spoke to Joseph day after day, but he refused.

While some scholars say that she was a sexually immoral woman with absolutely no discretion, others categorize her as one of the many bad girls of the Bible who are just scandalous in nature. However, when you study this fascinating story, you will discover an absentee husband who had more concern for the food in his belly than the wife in his home. Though he provided for his wife's material needs, her spiritual, emotional, and sexual needs were neglected. Companionship is more than a simple desire. It is an essential need. When it is missing within the confines of a relationship, it can lead to emptiness and a feeling of loneliness. Unfortunately, many spouses have turned into the arms of another when they've felt unwanted and unappreciated within their marriage. While the act of infidelity is totally reprehensible, it has become the common response of a neglected spouse.

Affair-Proof Your Marriage

Solution 1: Make A Covenant with Your Eyes

"What are you looking at?" yelled Tasha, as she saw her husband gazing at a petite, young woman walking across the street. "Nothing," sighed John, after hearing another accusation about the direction of his eyes. "I saw you lookin' at her! Don't stand here and lie to me. I'm sick and tired of you looking at some other woman every time I turn my head. Do you want her?"

This dialogue has become a common conversation amongst couples suffering from a spouse's wandering eyes. Whether it is the husband or the wife, this uncontrolled behavior has negatively affected many relationships. In fact, most one-night stands are birthed from a wandering, undisciplined eye. Unfortunately, this is not a recent phenomenon. Wandering, lustful eyes go back many centuries. So, to protect our marriages we must follow the same principle that Job understood and lived by:

"I made a covenant with my eyes not to look with lust upon a girl. I know full well that Almighty God above sends calamity on those who do. He sees everything I do, and every step I take. If I have lied and deceived - but God knows that I am innocent - or if I have stepped off God's pathway, or if my heart has lusted for what my eyes have seen, or if I am guilty of any other sin, then let someone else reap the crops I have sown and let all that I have planted be rooted out. Or if I have longed for another man's wife, then may I die, and may my wife be in another man's home, and someone else become her husband. For lust is a shameful sin, a crime that should be punished. It is a devastating fire that destroys to hell, and would root out all I have planted," Job 31:1-12.

Not only had Job avoided committing the great sin of adultery, but he managed to avoid taking the first step toward that sin by not looking at a woman with a lustful desire. What did Job understand that many of our men and women have yet to acknowledge? He understood that every form of sexual sin begins with a look.

Every eye gazer should recite Job's words before he starts his day. So, the next time you see that pretty, little secretary, or that suave corporate executive, you will know how to handle the situation. Besides, if it's not yours, why look anyway? Make a covenant with your eyes.

Solution 2: Avoid The Friendship Trap

One of the biggest questions couples struggle with is, *can men and women just be just friends?* This age-old question has gone unanswered which has created all types of problems in relationships. Interestingly, most emotional affairs are birthed within the confines of a platonic, opposite--sex friendship. How you may ask? Well, let's take a further look into the blurred lines of opposite--sex friends.

First, it must be stated that every relationship on the planet is based upon some form of attraction. That attraction may be emotional or physical. To attract means to have a liking for, or interest in something. It's very common for two people to be attracted to the same things- hobbies, sports, topics of conversation, etc. These are normal, everyday commonalities that naturally draw people to one another. So, if two members of the opposite sex have an appropriate shared interest, when and how does the relationship become inappropriate? When does an opposite-sex friendship cross the line? How do these friendships make a marriage vulnerable to an affair?

The following is an extensive list of Dave Carder's, "19 Signs of Close Call Friendships That Lead to an Affair." The purpose of these signs are to evaluate the degree to which one has wandered through the murky waters of an opposite-sex friendship and reached affair territory on the other side. These questions are early "red flag" indicators that one is either close to crossing, or has already crossed the line into an inappropriate relationship. The more checks, the more inappropriate the relationship. Do your best to be truthful as you check this list against your shared behaviors and feelings.

1. You save topics of conversation only for this friend.
2. You share spousal difficulties with them - a form of criticism towards your spouse.

3. Your friend shares his/her relationship difficulties with you.

4. You anticipate seeing your friend more than your spouse.

5. You begin comparing your spouse to your friend.

6. You show more concern about your friend than your spouse.

7. You provide special treats for your friend.

8. You fantasize about marriage with this friend.

9. You spend more time alone with this friend than your spouse.

10. Your spouse does not have access to all your conversations.

11. You spend money on your friend without your spouse's knowledge.

12. You begin having conflicts with your spouse over this friendship.

13. You lie to spend more time with this friend.

14. You hide interactions with your friend from your spouse.

15. You accuse your spouse of being jealous when he/she brings up the friendship.

16. You develop special rituals with your friend - which you both highly anticipate.

17. Your friend shares feelings or touches you and you inwardly respond - inner shiver.

18. Sexual content becomes a part of your conversations.

19. You do corporate dating - you are both participating in business travel for your company, church ministry, etc.- where you get entertained, eat, drink, and stay in the same hotel.

The aforementioned signs clearly describe what a platonic, opposite-sex friendship looks like. Unfortunately, most of society has been given the false impression that platonic is appropriate. On the contrary, it's highly inappropriate. The word platonic means intimate and affectionate, but not sexual. Intimacy and affection are behaviors that should be strictly reserved for a husband and wife. If you share any form of intimacy and affection with an opposite-sex friend, you are in the danger zone and an affair is probable. Therefore, it is important for you and your spouse to determine whether or not opposite-sex friends are appropriate for your marriage. If so, clear rules of engagement must be established in order to protect the sanctity of the marriage.

Solution 3: Overcome Your Sexual Addiction

Many spouses have allowed their flesh to control them. They have engaged in persistent and escalating patterns of sexual behavior, acting them out despite increasing consequences to themselves and others. They have used sex as a means to cope with problems or handle boredom, anxiety, and other powerful feelings. Some have used it as a way to feel important, wanted, or powerful.

Untamed sexual activities keep people in bondage. Most find themselves wrapped in a web of lies and manipulation, consistently hiding from those closest to them, while using justification, rationalization, and outright denial to lie to themselves. Sexual compulsion causes them to act in ways that go against their values and beliefs.

Even worse, many spouses with a flesh problem frequently say to themselves, "This is the last time that I am going to do that." However, they often find themselves feeling driven to return to the same sexual situations, despite previous commitments to change. Many are unable to make and keep commitments to themselves and others; they are unable to stop or change particular sexual behaviors long term. Instead, they continue to ride in the passenger seat down the fast lane of sexual sin, while lust recklessly drives at full force.

In order to truly conquer the sexual struggle, the first step that must be made is a quality decision to end all sexual behavior. However, you must first acknowledge your behavior as sin. Unfortunately, many people don't talk about sins today- they talk about problems. The reason that problems are more convenient than sins is because people don't have to do anything about them. If you have a problem, you can get sympathy, understanding, and even professional help for it. Sins, on the other hand, require repentance- to be confessed and forsaken. You can put away the sinful habits that have mastered you if you truly desire to do so, but you must accept personal responsibility for them. It is up to you to determine whether you're going to let your body be used for sin or for righteousness.

Next, a strategic multi-step plan must be properly executed. Too often, people take a one-dimensional, casual approach to recovery. They may read an article or two online, or possibly even a book educating them on symptoms associated with sexual addiction. While this may be helpful, it doesn't scratch the surface. The following steps must be taken.

1. Speak to a minister who can spiritually counsel you using the Word of God.
2. Seek professional help from someone who specializes in sex addiction recovery.
3. Join a weekly twelve-step support group, led by a specialist.
4. Find an accountability partner who can support you in your journey to recovery.
5. Establish a relationship with a mentor who has overcome sexual addiction.

This multi-step process will aid in your quest for the victory you desire in your life and marriage.

Solution 4: Reconnecting with Your Spouse

The language of attraction can become the language of seduction when communicated by the wrong person. When husbands and wives first meet, there is a natural attraction that occurs between the two. Relationships often begin with each person fascinated by the other's interests and pursuits. For instance, maybe you always hated opera, but now that you're dating an opera buff, you find yourself third-row-center and loving it. New love magically creates mutual interests.

Unfortunately, at some point, the desire to discover each other's passions tapers off. As your marriage matures, you become less focused on your partner's interests, refocusing on your own. There is less mutual activity and time spent together. Whether intentionally or by happenstance, individuals outside of the covenant begin to fill the voids created within the marriage. Once this happens, you must both plug up the holes and reclaim your marriage.

As a professional in marriage restoration, I've seen the power of quality time and recreational companionship in helping couples reclaim the emotional intimacy and connection that has been lost. Because of the closeness that shared activities bring, it is vital that you and your spouse carve out time for one another. There are different things a couple can do to deepen their emotional intimacy with one another. Finding what makes you and your spouse feel emotionally connected can go a long way toward strengthening your marriage. For more details on how you can reconnect with your spouse, read the chapter, "How to Create a Time-Rich Marriage."

Sexual fidelity is one of the most important symbols of commitment in a relationship. If you have not experienced infidelity in your marriage, look at this chapter as a precaution with warning signs to watch for. If you have experienced betrayal in your marriage, view this chapter as a roadmap to marital recovery. When we focus on making marriage our top priority, the entire family wins.

Couples Testimonial from
James & Roxanne Richards
Saint John's, Antigua and Barbuda

Earlier this year we had the privilege of having Hasani and Danielle Pettiford of Couples Academy travel all the way here to Antigua for our Marriage Retreat. We were amazed at passion and the wealth of information they offered. We've always had a great marriage but the weekend experience our marriage has been extraordinary. The other couples continue to testify about how their marriages have been transformed since the group intensive. We look forward to having Couples Academy back in Antigua in the near future.

chapter six

How to Heal
THE HURT
In Your Marriage

In the summer of 2015 I was staying at a fabulous hotel in Palms Springs, Florida for the weekend. The weather was great, the water was warm, and the food was amazing. Everything about the atmosphere was perfect, except for one thing- the reason for my trip. This was not the occasional romantic get-away that Danielle and I had become accustomed to; this was something very different.

Two weeks prior, I had received a distress call from a husband who had caught his wife in the act of adultery. He loved his wife, but he wasn't sure if his 10-year marriage could sustain the blow. He'd spent several weeks reading books, watching videos, meeting with his pastor, and searching the Internet for anything that could help to restore what was lost. After spending countless days filtering through hundreds of videos on our Couples Academy YouTube channel, he decided to pick up the phone and give me a call. A thirty-minute conversation later, my flight was booked and I began to prepare for another three-day private marriage intensive.

Most of my incoming distress calls center around

infidelity, but other complex issues prompt intervention as well. The issues are as diverse as the couples that I work with- from the woman who discovered that her husband was involved in a ten-year incestuous relationship with their daughter, to the traveling spouse who slept with twenty-three women while on tour. Or from the abusive marriage that began with repeated verbal threats and ended with guns drawn, to the couple with deep-seeded pain due to boundary-breaking in-laws.

These types of calls have become very common in our office. I receive them from both husbands and wives, whether they are newlyweds, married with small children, or empty-nesters. Regardless of their age, ethnicity, faith, tradition, or number of years married, couples continue to experience pain with no clear path of how to heal. In most cases, a book is not enough. A romantic couple's get-away just won't do. A marriage enrichment seminar doesn't dig deep enough and, as wise as your pastor may be, a two-hour counseling session can't address all of the issues. This pain calls for something more.

Most often, couples don't know what to do, so they do nothing and inevitably drift apart. Avoiding conflict is neither healthy, nor helpful, for any marriage. Often, we don't learn how to resolve marital conflict; instead we allow our problems to pile up. Over time, unresolved conflicts and unhealed hurts harden us, driving a wedge between husbands and wives.

Our three-day private marriage intensive allows us to resolve eighty percent of the problems impacting marriages. Couples often show up hurting, discouraged, and without hope. However, they leave feeling understood, validated, and encouraged about their future.

But, what happens when they get back home? Twenty percent of issues remain unresolved and must be dealt with. Even when those issues are resolved, emotional triggers and negative relational residue lingers. How do you deal with that? Does the pain ever go away? These are the questions that we're confronted with every day. To be honest, this is where the real work of Couples Academy begins.

A few years ago, I was contracted to be a resident expert for the nationally syndicated talk show, *The Bill Cunningham Show*. If you're unfamiliar with it, it falls in the same category of *The Jerry Springer Show* or *The Maury Povich Show*. The program's tagline was, 'Real People. Real Drama. Real Solutions.' One particular episode on which I appeared was entitled, "Tainted Scandalous Affairs."

The featured couple had experienced the pain of infidelity in their relationship and the offender couldn't understand why the hurt partner couldn't get over the pain. After the couple's back-and-forth feud, I was finally called upon to respond. Left with only 30 seconds to respond to their situation I stated to the gentleman...

"If I were to ball up my fist, punch you in the face and knock you on the floor, it would create a physical wound. It may take two hours to two days to heal from it. But, when you have certain behaviors and conduct in a relationship that are painful it can create emotional wounds which can take 2 months to 2 years to get over."

The audience immediately began to applaud. The response was so dramatic because people understood that recovering from betrayal is no small feat. It's not easy to 'just get over it.' In most cases the emotional pain inflicted on us by others can be far worse than any physical wound.

People can carry emotional scars with them for years because they never learn how to properly release them. As a result, those wounds continue to haunt and hurt. Whether they represent painful memories of the past, present day realities, or the anticipation of negative future outcomes, these issues can cripple lives and relationships.

According to relationship mathematics, we each have three core relationships that we must continually develop. The first relationship is the one we have with God. I call this our vertical relationship. The second is the personal relationship we have with ourselves. It is internal. The third is the relationship we have with a spouse. That is our horizontal relationship. Most marital discord results from neglect or the improper prioritization of one or more of these relationships.

If we truly want to be emotionally healed from past grievances, betrayals, and disappointments, we must do the work necessary to find healing in all three of the aforementioned relationships.

How to Get Past Your Past

Being joined together in marriage requires forgiveness, patience, and grace because no person is perfect, which ultimately means no marriage is perfect. We have all been recipient and contributor of emotional hurts and pains in marriage. None of us can make it in a marriage without experiencing some kind of pain.

The question is not, *what do you do IF you experience hurt in your marriage?* The question is, *what do you do WHEN you experience hurt in your marriage?* Whether the incident happened a few weeks, a few months, or even a few years ago, the ultimate question is, *how do you heal the hurt in your marriage when you are haunted by the ghosts of your past?*

We are all familiar with the biblical story of Lot and his wife. God placed judgment on Sodom and sent an angel to deliver a message to Lot: "Run for your lives! Don't look back. Run to the hills, so that you won't be killed." Unfortunately, Lot's wife disobeyed God and looked back on her past life and was turned into a pillar of salt. This clearly demonstrates that there is something destructive about becoming stuck looking at our past.

Several years ago, I coached a woman who had experienced something traumatic that continued to plague her relationships with family, friends, and co-workers. While at a retreat, I took her through an exercise that demonstrated the damage of dwelling on her past. I instructed her to stand at one end of a room and face the opposite end, which was approximately thirty feet away. Though the room housed several pieces of furniture, there was a path that led from one end of the room to the other.

I told her to imagine that the wall opposite her represented her future and the wall behind her represented her past. I then instructed her to walk toward her "future" wall. However, before taking her first step, I asked her to turn around and face her "past" wall and walk backwards toward her future. As she took a few steps back she bumped into a couch, then a chair, and then she stumbled over a coffee table. She quit her journey before making it to the other side of the room.

Immediately, she understood why she had spent the last three years living in pain. She realized that she had been looking at her future through the lenses of her past. Unfortunately, many of us who have experienced hurt in our marriage tend to live in the past and resist living in a new future. If our partner has lied, betrayed, or disappointed us, we are not quick to forget. Instead, we build walls with bricks made of anger, resentment, hostility, vindication, and un-forgiveness.

We often relive a past event over and over and over again, perhaps thousands of times, simply by thinking about it. Sometimes we're conscious of our thoughts, and sometimes we're not. Every time we replay that painful experience in our minds, we train our bodies to remember and experience the suffering all over again. After a while, we don't even have to think about the past event to create that feeling. We've got it memorized. We've created our own suffering and it's no longer our spouse hurting us. Instead, we are hurting ourselves by focusing on what our spouse has previously done, making it increasingly hard to have any hope for the future. As we begin to think about the future, we obsess over a worst-case scenario based on memories of our past, convincing ourselves that our spouse will never change.

Imagination begins to plan a future that reinforces the pain we are currently experiencing. The more we think about the possibility of our spouse cheating, lying, or hurting us, the more it negatively impacts our emotional state. Not only are we hurt by our past, we become frustrated and discouraged about our future and we convince ourselves of the probability of a negative outcome. This is damaging because we are programming our bodies to experience a painful event that hasn't yet happened. Then, rather than taking the time to embrace our present reality, we jump back and forth from a painful past to an anticipated painful future.

The only way to break this cycle and change our reality is to change the way we think, feel, and act. Romans 12:1 says, "Do not conform to the pattern of this world, but be transformed by the renewing of your mind..." In other words, we must think differently. If we renew our minds with a new way of thinking, we will break the patterns that have trapped us in our own pain. Because our minds are both records of the past and roadmaps to the future, we must leave our past in the past and anticipate a better future. When we have negative, fearful, or impatient thoughts, we begin to feel negative, fearful, and impatient. Likewise, when we have great, loving, and joyous thoughts we produce chemicals that make us feel great, loving, or joyful.

We should use our bodies as tools that serve us. Instead of obsessing about some painful event that we fear is waiting for us, we must obsess about something good. Obsess about a new, desirable experience that we can wrap our emotions around. See and experience the marriage you want, not the one you have. See your spouse doing the right thing, not all the wrong previously done. See a better version of yourself, not the same person you've always been. Live in a new future, and as you begin to believe that you're experiencing the elevated emotions of a new future outcome in the present moment, you transform. You become more hopeful, optimistic, and willing to work on the restoration of your marriage.

The True Path of Forgiveness

Forgiveness is one of the greatest blessings that God has given us, and one of the greatest blessings we can give to others. Throughout time, people of all faith traditions have been taught the principle, purpose, and power of forgiveness. What has remained missing from the teaching is the proper application of forgiveness. As a result, we remain trapped in a relationship full of pain and agony.

If you think you have been wronged so badly that you can't forgive when someone apologizes and genuinely repents, then consider Jesus' own story. After living with His chosen disciples, traveling with them, performing miracles in front of them, and even dying for them, Peter denied knowing Him- three times. Ouch! You know that betrayal must have hurt Jesus terribly.

Fortunately, after doing this, Peter was filled with regret and sadness. He wept bitterly from his sin and repented. Jesus forgave him. Peter went on to be a great apostle for Christ and, in fact, Christ trusted Peter to establish God's church. Wow. That is true forgiveness. Now, knowing the principle and power of forgiveness, let's take a look at its proper application by exploring four areas.

1) Un-forgiveness
2) Cheap forgiveness
3) Acceptance
4) True forgiveness

They each have their own set of characteristics and behaviors. It's important to know what to do and what not to do in order to truly forgive. Let's explore the path of true forgiveness together.

Un-forgiveness

Denying someone forgiveness when they have hurt us can become an automatic response. Truthfully speaking, there are many of us for whom a refusal to forgive is a lifelong response pattern. We are grudge holders, with a past full of damaging life experiences and negative feelings toward forgiveness. We are easily offended, less empathetic and often vengeful. In fact, it is quite common to find a broken trail of relationships beginning in childhood.

Even though our refusal to forgive hurts, it feels better to offer no opportunity for someone to repay their debt. It feels better to show them that what they did was unforgivable. It feels better to punish them. However, if we all lived by the mantra "an eye for an eye and tooth for a tooth," we would all be blind and toothless. James Baldwin once said, "I imagine one of the reasons people cling to their hate so stubbornly is because they sense that once hate is gone they will be forced to deal with the pain."

You want your pain understood and validated, but that can't come by punishing your partner. You have to let go of the rage because, while it may give voice to your pain, it will not help your hurt feelings. Instead, your wounds will remain unhealed. The gratification one gets through un-forgiveness is short-lived and the "feel good" we get from it is not real. When you deny forgiveness, what started as self-protection ends up leaving you feeling cold and bitter. It may seem attractive, but it turns out to be maladaptive in a number of ways. First, un-forgiveness denies both you and your spouse the possibility of reconciliation, leaving you stuck.

Second, un-forgiveness cuts you off from any

opportunity for personal growth and understanding- the opportunity to look inward and learn to change. It may restore your pride, but when you refuse to forgive, you transfer blame to the offender, making yourself faultless. It is really a refusal to question how you may be wrong. It serves as a tool to help you escape the fear of facing your own failures.

Finally, un-forgiveness poisons you physically and emotionally. It leaves you detached from life, cut off from tenderness, beauty, and joy. Things that should be pleasurable are tainted by rage, making you obsessed with getting even. You fail to satisfy your needs for peace, creativity, love, and connection. So many negative emotions racing through you may make you feel physically sick and more susceptible to illness.

Cheap Forgiveness

Cheap Forgiveness is quick and easy, with no processing of emotions or coming to terms with the pain. It is unhealthy because it creates the illusion of True Forgiveness. Unfortunately, when nothing has been resolved, by silencing your anguish and indignation, you fail to acknowledge the harm that has been done to you. Offering quick clemency stunts personal and relational growth. When you forgive too quickly, you fail to learn the lessons that help you develop healthy, lasting relationships and refusal to confront issues gives your partner validation in their mistreatment of you.

Cheap Forgiveness comes in different forms. Conflict Avoidance is the most common. It dismisses an injury for the sake of protecting a relationship. No matter how you feel beneath the surface, you act as though nothing is wrong. You remain in a relationship without a voice and without any sense of entitlement. Often, your silence is linked to fear-fear that your partner will retaliate with anger or violence, fear of rejection or abandonment, or fear that speaking up for yourself will harm your spouse.

Moral Superiority is another form of Cheap Forgiveness. You forgive quickly, glossing over the issues, which makes you feel like you are a better person than the offender. However, it prevents you and your partner from getting closer. Ask yourself if your forgiveness is an act of humility or a manipulation meant to establish superiority. If it is the latter, you rob yourself of the opportunity to have the offender tend to your wounds and make you feel cared for.

Acceptance

Acceptance is a response to a violation that takes place when the person who hurt you is either unavailable or unrepentant. An unavailable person can be someone for whom you may still be harboring negative emotions for who has passed away. It also applies to someone you no longer have relationship with or have a way of communicating with. An unrepentant person would be a person with whom you are in relationship, but that refuses to comply with the forgiveness process.

Nonetheless, you feel the need to forgive for your own personal healing. You may not be responsible for the harm that was done to you, but you are responsible for your recovery. For example, if you are sitting in a chair minding your business and I walk up to you and knock you onto the floor, that is my fault. However, if I come back a week later and you are in the same spot crying and complaining about being knocked down, that is your fault. In no way does this underestimates the necessary grieving and recovery process one must go through, but your offender may never come to your aid. So, either you stay on the ground, or you pick yourself up. By picking yourself up, you heal yourself, thereby gaining the ability to make peace and the potential to restore your relationship. Acceptance is when you give up the need for revenge and instead, you continue to seek resolution.

In order to truly embrace acceptance, you must frame your spouse's behavior as an outward expression of his or her own personal weakness or struggle. This does not excuse the behavior, but it frees you from the notion that the behavior was done with the intent to harm you. Even though the impact of your spouse's behavior may be destructive to you and the family, most likely their focus has more to do with their personal gain than your personal loss. Here are a few things to seriously consider when embracing acceptance:

1. Look inward. Often we create our own rage, fed by our personalities, provocations, and exaggerated responses to conflict. While your partner may have done something to offend, perhaps it is not as bad as your response suggests.

2. Challenge assumptions about what happened. Sometimes, we forget to distinguish our version of the truth from reality. Separating the facts of what actually happened, versus what we think happened, is a critical part of the acceptance process. You may find that your pain is grounded in misunderstanding.

3. Look at your partner as a whole person, not just as the offender. Don't look exclusively at the moment of the mistreatment. Rather, look at all of the moments you have shared. Take caution to be true to your memories, not letting one obliterate the rest.

4. Forgive yourself. You may need to forgive yourself for blindly trusting, for having a stunted view of yourself, and for feeling entitled to loyalty and love. You may need to forgive yourself for self-destructive behaviors, such as belittling your suffering, believing you got what you deserved, viewing your mistreatment as punishment, or for allowing it to shatter and shame you. You may need to forgive yourself for tolerating abusive behavior, making peace at all costs, or for losing time and energy engaging in vindictive dialogues. Finally, you may need to forgive yourself for your own bad behavior that has contributed your pain. Minimizing or ignoring your actions will keep you trapped in a world of un-forgiveness and will ensure that the cycle of bad behavior will continue. Instead, look introspectively and commit to personal change.

True Forgiveness

True Forgiveness is a healing process you commit to with your partner in which both parties make the effort to heal. It is a transaction, not an all-inclusive pardon granted by the hurt party. It's an exchange between the two of you and it comes with conditions. True Forgiveness must be earned. The offender must be willing to pay the price. In exchange, the hurt party must allow the debt to be paid. As the offender works hard to earn forgiveness, the hurt party works hard to let go of resentment. If either party fails to do the work, there can be no True Forgiveness.

For the offender, true repentance is the best way to begin earning forgiveness and it is rarely ever as simple as saying, "I'm sorry". It is much more than just acknowledging wrongdoing. It is a change of mind and heart that gives us a fresh view of the marriage and ourselves. It includes turning away from destructive behaviors and turning toward God.

One of the things that hold individuals back from receiving forgiveness is the feeling that they don't deserve to be forgiven. Sadly, this will ensure that forgiveness will be withheld. This belief will cause a person to engage in self-sabotaging behaviors, creating more problems. So, you must accept that you are truly worthy of forgiveness. Only then can you accept true forgiveness from God, your spouse, and yourself.

Next, you must take the time to recognize the pain you've caused. Ask your spouse to open up to you and truly listen. Until the hurt party releases the pain they feel, you will not be able to obtain forgiveness. You have to be willing to face what you've done and see it from a different perspective. Getting your spouse to open up to you may not be an easy task. They may forgive too easily in order to avoid conflict, while continuing to rage inside. At first, silence may seem preferable to rage, but don't be fooled. Hidden pain is just as devastating to a marriage as uncontrolled fury. Avoiding the original problem does not make it disappear. Instead, it widens the gap between spouses.

Surprisingly, controlled conflict creates closeness. In order to rebuild your bond, you must be willing to go into uncharted waters, even if they seem dangerous. Too often, offenders aren't willing to deal with hot button issues. They would rather avoid discussions at all cost. Why? They want to avoid the inevitable conflict that arises when the topic emerges. Unfortunately, there are no short cuts or alternative ways around this process. I tell my clients all the time that they've got to be willing to get dirty and deal with all of the outstanding issues in order to truly move forward. They've got to continuously encourage their partner to reveal the depth of their pain. Opening up is an act of intimacy. It's a major step towards lowering the barrier that exists in the relationship.

When the violation is brought up, you must let the hurt party know that you have not forgotten what was done, that you are learning from it, and that you want to help them heal. A person cannot forgive you if you're indifferent to their suffering. Then, look inside to try and understand your behavior. Reveal the truth you discover to your partner and then work to regain trust. Forgive yourself for hurting someone you care about. Then, genuinely, sincerely apologize. Some guidelines for forming an appropriate apology are:

- Take responsibility for the pain you caused. You must acknowledge your role. Don't throw out an apology that downplays your responsibility, such as, "I'm sorry if I hurt your feelings." An effective apology is an acknowledgement that you were wrong.

- Make your apology personal, not just an admission that you did something wrong. In helping your partner to heal and move forward, you must show you care about having violated them.
- Make your apology specific. Don't just offer a generic, "I'm sorry," or an, "I'm sorry for whatever I did." Apologize not only for hurting the person you love, but for how you hurt them. Build trust by recognizing the specific harm that you caused.
- Make assurances to never cross that line again. Being truly apologetic means, not only feeling bad about what you did, but striving not to make the same mistake in the future.
- Make your apology sincere. Don't apologize only to satisfy your guilt or get out of trouble. Avoid an apology like, "I said I was sorry...what else do you want," "I'm sorry for stepping on your big fat ego," or "I know I'm in the doghouse unless I say sorry, so there it is." Your apology will likely fall on deaf ears if your heart isn't in it. You want to convey a transformation of heart. Use appropriate tone of voice, body language, attitude, and words. Be gentle and warm, make eye contact, and stay focused.
- Apologize repeatedly. Often, especially for more serious injuries, a single apology is not viewed as the same as actually being apologetic. Being apologetic means to offer an apology as often as it is needed, to carry the sorrow with you until your partner is able to let it go, and to not be resentful of having to offer multiple regrets.

- Do not deny, discount, or dismiss the injury. Most importantly, do not try to make your partner feel guilty for needing an apology.

God Is in the Healing Business

Complete restoration is experienced when you chase after God. There is one place you can always turn for healing. That place is in the presence of the Lord. The Bible has clearly established that He is able to meet emotional needs. In the presence of God we find rest, peace of mind, a softened heart, and hope for the future. He is able to heal the emotional wounds of rejection, abandonment, abuse, neglect, insecurity, embarrassment, shame, un-forgiveness, and all other deeply imbedded pains. When these wounds continue to fester and flare up, God guarantees total recovery.

The following scriptures indicate God's ability to completely heal every emotional hurt and pain.

"The Spirit of the Sovereign LORD is on me, because the LORD has...sent me to bind up the brokenhearted, to proclaim freedom for the captives...to comfort all who mourn... to bestow on them a crown of beauty instead of ashes, the oil of joy instead of mourning, and a garment of praise instead of a spirit of despair." Isaiah 61:1-3

"He will wipe away every tear from their eyes, and death shall be no more, neither shall there be mourning, nor crying, nor pain anymore, for the former things have passed away." Revelation 21:4

"He heals the brokenhearted and binds up their wounds."
Psalm 147:3

"Cast your burden on the LORD, and he will sustain you; he
will never permit the righteous to be moved." Psalm 55:22

"Come to me, all who labor and are heavy laden, and I will
give you rest. Take my yoke upon you, and learn from me, for
I am gentle and lowly in heart, and you will find rest for your
souls. For my yoke is easy, and my burden is light." Matthew
11:28-30

These promises of emotional healing are available to all
who desire them. However, there is one caveat- God's
promises are always conditional. They require partnership.
God is saying, "if you do this…then I will do that." This is a
very important note to consider. Many believers take a
passive, laid back, do-nothing approach to recovery.
Unfortunately, they believe if they throw God a quick prayer
then He will take care of the rest. God does not operate like
that. We must pray as if everything depends on God, but
work as if everything depends on us. We must take an
account of every one of our concerns and then turn them
over to Him. Now, once we hand them over we must make
an internal vow never to take them back. God will deal with
them so we no longer have to. Once we give them over to
God the bible tells us that He will provide us with whatever
is needed. Matthew 11:29 says, "Come to me, take my yoke
upon you and learn from me."

In other words, get in the presence of God through your
personal time of study, prayer, and meditation. It then says

take his yoke upon you. A yoke is a bar or frame that is attached to the heads or necks of two work animals (such as oxen) so that they can pull a plow or heavy load. Imagine being yoked up with Jesus. Your heads are connected to one another (taking on the mind of Christ). It then says learn from me. The more you learn about the power of Christ, the more you learn about yourself. The more you discover who you really are, the more those life-long issues begin to drop off one by one.

Personal healing is at your fingertips. Life and marital transformation comes from a lifestyle of consistent behavior. By exercising the techniques mentioned here- well beyond your season of healing- you can ensure that you never wind up in painful, unfulfilled place again.

Couples Testimonial from
Marcus & Nicole Brown
Los Angeles, California

After dating for seven years, we got married thinking that our "love" was enough. Four years later, we were headed towards divorce. Trying to choose from a long list of counselors' online whom we've never met, was difficult. Having a college degree doesn't guarantee they're any good. Hasani Pettiford has a God given talent that education can't buy. He has an intuitive nature to pick on emotions unspoken. His ability to communicate those emotions felt by each of us, were clear, simple and made us feel comfortable. Through this experience we know and understand each other on a deeper level. We're closer now than any other time in our entire eleven years together. Hasani has given us a toolbox full of survival skills to last us a lifetime.
We thank God for him! Thank you!

Place Your Marriage On The Path To Fulfillment
With CouplesAcademy.org

COUPLES ACADEMY
PUBLICATIONS

chapter seven

How to Create
A TIME RICH
M a r r i a g e

Do you sometimes feel as though you barely know your spouse? Have your lives become filled with tasks, duties, and responsibilities, instead of activities that create real intimacy? If so, you are not alone.

Many couples fall victim to this reality. A subtle change that happens over time, usually involves becoming fully invested in activities outside of the relationship. Sadly, couples tend to transition from through stages: (1) soulmates, to (2) role-mates, to (3) roommates. When you don't invest time in your marriage, an emotional disconnect inevitably occurs. This disconnect is often detrimental to the success of the marriage. The transition from a happy and fulfilling marriage, to an unfulfilling one usually occurs in three steps.

First, couples start out as soulmates, which is often experienced during the "honeymoon phase." In this stage of marriage, you have great communication with your partner. There is no lack of emotional intensity or sexual fulfillment. You are the best of friends and the loves of each other's lives. Couples in this stage often hold hands, exchange kisses, and enjoy small and comfortable public displays of affection. They routinely make time for conversation, companionship, and intimacy. However, while this behavior is natural in the beginning of the relationship, it tends to diminish over time.

If you are not intentional in your efforts to keep the passion alive, your relationship may slip into the next phase, which is an undesirable one: role-mates. In this phase you are no longer companions; you are strictly partners. You remain partners in responsibilities such as raising children, managing finances, and maintaining the upkeep of the home, but the emotional connection you once shared is no longer alive. Everything becomes about responsibilities and obligations. Often, when children come along the relationship further corrodes. Many couples make the mistake of taking off their "husband" and "wife" hats, replacing them with "daddy" and "mommy" hats. In fact, many totally neglect their original roles as partners, solely becoming parents. The love, physical affection, emotional connection, and quality time that they once gave each other becomes exclusively devoted to the children.

Often, when children are not the cause of the marital decline, devotion to activities outside the home becomes the culprit. For instance, activities such as work, church, and volunteering are pushed to the top of our priority lists. These activities aren't bad; in fact, they are socially endorsed and considered good. However, when more time is invested in them than in the marriage, couples begin to pull away from each other. All of a sudden spouses co-exist. Once that happens the marriage is in trouble.

If the dynamics of the marriage don't change, a couple can begin to sink into an even more deplorable role:

roommates. In this stage, all signs of a healthy relationship are non-existent. Unfortunately, the only things binding the couple together are children and finances. Husbands and wives go their separate ways in every other aspect of marriage.

Does any of this sound familiar? Can you identify which category you and your partner fall into? If you are in the role-mate or roommate category, you may feel like all hope is lost. It's not. You can get back to being soul-mates. It will take hard work, dedication, and a pro-active attitude. Most importantly, it will take time. It will be difficult, but it will be worth it.

Danielle and I have experienced all three of these stages. Like most couples, our soulmate phase was short lived. We teetered back and forth between role-mates and roommates. Our inability to navigate our way back to soulmates after being hit with so much, so quickly- the combination of small children, financial challenges, personality conflicts, and feelings of abandonment due to long working hours- almost destroyed our marriage. In coping with the pressures of life, our personal relationship became the last thing on our list of priorities. I buried myself in work, leaving Danielle to deal with the complexities of life alone. Even though we dwelled in the same house, we lived separate lives. I was often physically there, but mentally and emotionally checked out. Over time, Danielle became resentful and consumed by feelings of abandonment.

Danielle's number one complaint at this point was that I never spent time with her and the kids. She would say, "You're always in your office, on the computer, inside the pages of a book, or scrolling through your phone." I realized that I was guilty of one of the most serious sins of all failed marriages: neglect. When you neglect your spouse, you provide them with inadequate attention, usually resulting from a carelessness or disregard for the needs of your partner. Not only had I neglected her emotionally, but I had neglected her physically as well. I was never around, and I had no idea what long-term impact my behavior would have on my marriage.

Galatians 6:7 says, "Do not be deceived: God is not mocked, for whatever one sows, that will he also reap." I sowed the seeds of neglect and reaped a harvest of loveless-ness. After a long awaited, five-hour conversation, I realized that if things didn't drastically change, divorce was inevitable. I'd spent years putting people's marriages back together, while simultaneously tearing mine apart. I had been emotionally invested in the lives of others, while being emotionally divested from my own family. It became apparent that there was only one way to turn my marriage and family around. It required a huge investment of my time.

The Time-Starved Marriage

We've all heard of sex starved marriages, but time starved marriages aren't as widely recognized. Nevertheless, a tremendous number of couples suffer from a lack of quality time spent together. In fact, in a national survey, researchers found that the average couple engages in approximately four minutes of meaningful conversation a day. Sadly, that time is split between the two most stressful times of the day: (1) when they are on their way to work, and (2) when they are on their way back from an exhausting day of work. Neither of these is a time when anyone is at their best. Meanwhile, people spend eight to ten hours a day communicating with co-workers, customers, and colleagues. Unfortunately, deeper and more meaningful relationships are often developed at work, rather than at home. Many of us are guilty of giving the world our best selves. We are attentive, engaging, involved, and interested. By time we get home, we're exhausted, giving our spouses only what's left over.

Imagine pulling left over trays of food from the refrigerator, scraping together the remains that are stuck to the edges of a pan, and serving this up as a meal. As you throw the paper plate of food on the table directly in front of your spouse, you sarcastically say, "Bon Appetit." As insensitive as that sounds, that is exactly what we are doing when we give our partners the scraps that are left over after our day. Over commitment, exhaustion, and busyness are silent killers that destroy marriages. This phenomenon, also known as sunset fatigue, is when a person is too drained, too tired, or too preoccupied to be fully present with their spouse. They give what's left over and, unfortunately, a marriage cannot survive on leftovers for too long. Marriages require quality time.

For more than a decade I have met with couples who have experienced major crises in their marriages- infidelity, incest, domestic violence, the death of a child, and impending divorce. I've seen couples bounce back from some of the most daunting situations. I have watched major breakthroughs and transformations. The area that couples struggle with most is their time investment in one another. Whether we are overcommitted, working long hours, or available but not interested, we are all guilty of a gross mismanagement of our time. We justify this by telling ourselves that we don't have the time. While we claim that our marriages and families are the most important priorities in our lives, we can't find the time to invest in either of them. So, they suffer as a result.

Our gross mismanagement of time and its devastating implications are perfectly articulated in Roman philosopher Lucius Seneca's book, *On the Shortness of Life*. Read it slowly in order grasp the depths of his words:

> *"It is not that we have a short space of time, but that we waste much of it. Life is long enough, and it has been given in sufficiently generous measure to allow the accomplishment of the very greatest things, if the whole of it is well invested. But when it is squandered in luxury and carelessness, when it is devoted to no good end, forced at last by the ultimate necessity, we perceive that it has passed away before we were aware that it was passing. So it is- the life we receive is not short, but we make it so; nor do we have any lack of it, but are wasteful of it. Just as great and princely wealth is scattered in a moment when it comes into the hands of a bad owner, while wealth, however limited, if it is entrusted to a good guardian, increases by use, so our life is amply long for him who orders it properly."*

Essentially, when both spouses make the decision to prioritize their relationship, the success of their marriage is inevitable. The only way to become soulmates again is through the proper management of time.

relationship than problems within the bedroom. When a couple first weds they experience the "Honeymoon Effect". This is a state of perpetual passion and bliss in which you and your spouse are head over heels in love with each other. Life is beautiful and you can't wait to wake up each morning to spend time together.

Often, within that same year, disillusionment settles in. Why? Expectations aren't being met. The kind of care you assume you are going to be receiving isn't provided. The conflict stage arrives, comprised of fights and disagreements. Due to poor communication and inadequate conflict management skills, issues go unresolved and couples begin to disconnect emotionally. The highly intensified feelings of love and passion begin to dissipate and the first thing that is affected within the marriage is sex. When conflict and disappointment begin to rear their ugly heads, they must be effectively addressed and resolved immediately. If either or both partners lack the necessary skills to resolve the problem, it is recommended to seek outside help in order to ensure the success of the relationship.

Sex is an amazing gift given by God for couples who dwell within a covenant relationship. When we come together and unify mentally, emotionally, and sexually we honor God and his system for marriage.

Couples Testimonial from
Patricia & Darrell White
West Orange, New Jersey

From the very beginning, Hasani has made me feel at ease with ALL of the issues, concerns, anxieties, fears etc. my mate and I were experiencing. His methodical approach to tackling each issue is one I have never experienced before. Hasani hones in on each area of concern and will not move forward until there is a level of clear understanding. My time with him has been extremely rewarding. However, please don't get me wrong, this journey is no walk in the park. There are assignments and reading that must be completed in preparation for upcoming sessions. He expects you to put in 100% as he is surely putting in 100%. If I ever have a question or a concern, all I have to do is reach out to him, and I am guaranteed a response. I have NEVER experienced a counselor/ coach to be as dedicated to their clients as Hasani. His passion for his client's success reassures me that I have made the right decision.

chapter ten

Change Your Life
CHANGE
Your Marriage

In the summer of 2014, Couples Academy was in the midst of an identity crisis. Danielle and I had always had a heart for marriage. Helping couples become more passionate in their partnerships was our greatest desire. We dedicated much of our time to hosting couples retreats, facilitating workshops, and offering coaching services to couples wanting to enhance their already stable relationships.

Our tagline was great: 'Placing Couples on the Path to Fulfillment'. It sounded great. It looked great. It felt great. Unfortunately, there was one major problem- it no longer worked great. After relocating our entire family to Atlanta, Georgia, we discovered that our country was in the midst of a marriage crisis. Infidelity, domestic violence, separation, and divorce were at all-time highs. Couples were no longer interested in romantic getaways, group date nights, or cozy social gatherings. Marriage enrichment was no longer a priority. All over the nation, couples were in crisis and needed real help.

After receiving multiple phone calls, emails, and text messages, we quickly discovered that couples did not need to be placed on the path to fulfillment; instead, they needed a road to recovery. All of the requests we received were desperate pleas for marriage help. It was at that moment that Danielle and I made the executive decision to change the focus of the company. Couples Academy would become "The Home of Infidelity Recovery and Divorce Prevention". For this identity shift, I immediately sought training as an Infidelity Recovery Specialist.

This shift opened the floodgates. We went from having a small, local coaching office, to establishing a global brand. In addition to serving the greater Atlanta area, requests began to come in from New York City, Chicago, Los Angeles, Houston, Mexico, Toronto, London, Antigua, Bangkok, and Dubai. I am still amazed at how God has positioned us to make an impact on marriages and families around the world.

Even with all of the differences in culture, language, and faith, I quickly discovered one common thread among marital conflict. When couples are in conflict, each partner shifts the blame, exonerating him or herself of any wrongdoing. During our initial 30-minute discovery session, the narrative always winds up being the same. 'My spouse is the problem...He doesn't do his fair share around the house...She no longer meets my sexual needs...If he doesn't change I'm filing for divorce...This is my last chance getting her to see the error of her ways...'

The list goes on and on and on. The only change that people are committed to is the change they want to see in their spouse. As a coach/counselor in this situation, clients leave me with two options- either fix their spouse, or help them get a divorce and get out of their doomed marriage. So,

I let them vent for 20 minutes and then I typically respond with the following statement:

"If you are sick and tired of your marriage and ready to get a divorce, by all means, DO IT! Why stay in a broke, miserable, and unfulfilled relationship? Who wants that? We all deserve to be happy. When Danielle and I were at the point of calling it quits, I wanted to get a divorce, and that's exactly what I did.

I divorced myself from my own negativity, poor communication habits, pompous ego, irrational convictions, and deeply embedded beliefs that worked against my marriage. When I made the decision to 'DIVORCE ME FROM MYSELF' it saved my marriage. So, rather than divorcing your partner, DIVORCE YOU. Then, and only then, will you begin to have the marriage you truly desire. Remember, your spouse is not the only problem, your shortcomings are also your problem. Work on that and your marriage will SOAR!!!"

Usually, after about thirty seconds of silence, the desperate spouse awkwardly clears their throat and says, "Well alright then. What's the next step and how do we get started?" I help them realize that the problems they see in their spouse may be the very issues they are hiding within themselves. When relationships become rocky, or fail altogether, it is easy to blame the other person's flaws. Pointing a finger is far easier than self-examination. If you recognize that all of your relationships, romantic or otherwise, serve as mirrors of yourself, you begin to realize that these flaws are present in you, too. Getting angry or irritated after recognizing flaws in someone else usually means that you are denying their existence within yourself. You are not fully accepting the bad with the good.

With personalities on opposite ends of the spectrum, we find things in our significant others that we would give anything to change. When we focus on them, they seem to grow, expand, and become more irritating. However, when we take our eyes off of our partners and place them on ourselves, their issues seem to dissipate. Keeping our eyes focused on our partner's flaws keeps us stuck in a pattern of negativity.

Do You Have a Groundhog Marriage?

Ground Hog Day is a movie about an arrogant TV weatherman named Phil Connors- played by Bill Murray- who is sent to the town of Punxsutawney to cover an event called Groundhog Day. At first, everything seems normal as he covers the event, but then he wakes up the next day and realizes something is wrong- it's yesterday all over again! He's stuck in a time loop and no one else seems to be aware.

After Phil realizes that the day is repeating itself, he is very confused, then frustrated. He goes through several negative stages. He becomes hedonistic, criminal, depressed, opportunistic, suicidal, and downright cynical. He robs banks, cons people, and even tries to seduce his love interest to no avail. His attitude and behavior take him on a downward spiral.

No matter what he does, he can't escape the time loop and the next day is the same day all over again. He becomes dejected and eventually confides in someone, which brings him to an "aha" moment. Phil realizes that if he's going to be stuck in this time loop, he might as well make the best of it.

The next day, Phil wakes up a changed man. He starts to

care about others and he adopts a keen curiosity for life. One evening, while at a diner, he hears a piano piece and is mesmerized by it. He takes up piano classes and becomes a master pianist. He goes around the town helping people and, thanks to the time loop, knows exactly when and where to appear in order to save everyone. He becomes a genuinely good-hearted, altruistic person who serves humanity. Phil's decision to change his life changed his circumstances. His personal transformation breaks the time loop ensnaring him. He wakes up to a day that is no longer February 2nd. Finally, it is the next day, February 3rd.

The big question is, *how many days did Phil live the same day?* Fans all over the world have been trying to figure that out for years. Most people believe that he lived 38 separate days in the movie. However, through further analysis and deep interpretation, it has been concluded that Phil Connor spent 12,395 days locked in Groundhog Day. That's a resounding total of 33 years and 350 days.

Can you imagine being trapped in a miserable marriage for over 33 years? Unfortunately, many of us don't have to imagine. We've been stuck in the time loop of a horrible marriage for a long time. Are you in a marital time loop? How long has it been? One year? 10 years? Twenty-five years? However long it may be, you can break it once and for all. You can become unstuck in your relationship; you only have to make a decision.

So, what does it mean to be stuck in a relationship? It means to be unchanging, unwilling to move forward in the marriage. Many people assume that it only takes one to be stuck in a relationship, but it takes two. If one spouse is unwilling to change, they are contributing to the problem just as much as the spouse that is sitting in the seat of judgment and blame. Unfortunately, couples become stuck in patterns they've gotten used to over time, making it hard to become unstuck. The longer you remain in that state, the more resentful you become, which can cause feelings of hopelessness. The good news is, even though it takes two to become stuck in a bad marriage, it only takes one to break the pattern and get out of the loop. Just keep one thing in mind: It is a simple process, but it is not easy. Making changes to our personal lives is never an easy task, but it is doable. It will require work, because that's what marriage is. I often say that marriage is spelled W-O-R-K because in order to have a successful marriage, unyielding effort is required.

Through much research, psychologists have concluded that by the time we reach our mid-thirties, our personality is completely formed. For those of us over the age of thirty-five, we have memorized a select set of behaviors, beliefs, attitudes, emotional reactions, habits, memories, perceptions and conditioned responses that are subconsciously programmed within us. Simply put, we generally think the same thoughts, feel the same feelings, react the same ways, behave in the same manners, believe the same precepts, and perceive reality the same ways. Much like a computer that is operated by software running in the background, there are programs running us. In fact, about ninety-five percent of who we are is a series of subconscious programs that have become automatic.

The reason we struggle with change is because we've memorized a set of behaviors so well that we have become automatic beings. It has been concluded by the scientific community that five percent of our mind is conscious and struggling against the ninety-five percent that is running subconsciously. So, ninety-five percent of our day, though we appear to be awake, we are actually unconscious.

Think about that. A person may consciously want to be happy and fulfilled within their marriage, but they suffer the repeated cycle of pain, misery, bitterness, and un-forgiveness due to years of conditioning. When we engage in a thought or behavior long enough, it no longer requires intention; it becomes instinctual. Unfortunately, many of us are living life based upon a set of memorized habits that don't serve us. We are no longer aware of what we are thinking, doing, or feeling. We have become unconscious, leaving a large percentage of our marriages to autopilot.

I often sit in sessions where couples fight about what was said and done. One spouse will do something one minute, and then swear up and down that they didn't do it. How is this possible? Are they living in denial? Are they lying to their partner and to themselves? Possibly. Or, perhaps, they have been doing or saying something for so long that they've become unaware of their own behavior. They are living life unconsciously.

I counsel so many couples that are fed up with being stuck. Like them, we all want more for our lives and relationships. We all come to a point when we realize change is necessary. However, every time we decide to trust again, to open up and believe again, our internal systems go into chaos. Like a drug, our bodies have become addicted to the negative thoughts and emotions that keep us trapped in our own miserable conditions. We fall victim to an internal conversation that presents a multitude of reasons that we should not change our current behavior. The more we think about the issues, the more we feel justified in our decision to remain cautious, distant, and unwilling to trust. Over time, we unconsciously condition our minds and bodies to operate in self-sabotaging behaviors that keep us from experiencing the very thing we truly desire- a fulfilling marriage.

Political activist Stokely Carmichael once said, "The job of the conscious is to make the unconscious aware of their unconscious behavior, thus making them conscious." Put another way, when we become aware of our unconscious behavior, we are able to make the necessary changes in all areas of our lives. Author James Allen said, "Men are anxious to improve their circumstances, but are unwilling to improve themselves; they, therefore, remain bound." This means, we may want to improve our careers, but we are unwilling to improve ourselves. We may want to improve our finances, but we are unwilling to improve ourselves. We may even want to improve our marriages, but we are unwilling to improve ourselves. Carmichael and Allen are saying that if we want our circumstances to change, the change must first begin within us. It requires that we become aware of our habits and break them.

We're all creatures of habit, whether we like it or not. A habit is something we do so often it becomes easy. It's a behavior that we repeat until it produces a result. We can make a habit our servant, or we can allow it to become our master. The choice is ours. The power of habits is eloquently explained in the following poem:

I am your constant companion.
I am your greatest helper or your heaviest burden.
I will push you onward or drag you down to failure.
I am completely at your command.
Half the things you do, you might just as well turn over to me,
And I will be able to do them quickly and correctly.
I am easily managed; you must merely be firm with me.
Show me exactly how you want something done,
And after a few lessons I will do it automatically.
I am the servant of all great men.
And, alas, of all failures as well.
Those who are great, I have made great
Those who are failures, I have made failures.
I am not a machine, though I work with all the precision
of a machine
Plus, the intelligence of a man.
You may run me for profit, or run me for ruin;
It makes no difference to me.
Take me, train me, be firm with me
And I will put the world at your feet.
Be easy with me, and I will destroy you.
Who am I?
I am HABIT

–Unknown Author

The great news is that you can change your habits any time you choose. Breaking bad habits and replacing them with good ones is extremely important because they play a major role in how the future of your relationship unfolds.

The Key to Lasting Change

In order to truly transform your marriage, you must follow one key principle. According to veteran actor Dondre Whitfield, "You must model the behavior you want your spouse to mirror." In essence, change yourself first. It's easy to point the finger and focus on the shortcomings of your spouse. No effort is required with that. However, I caution you to realize that every time you point the finger at your partner, there are three fingers pointing back at you. That implies that you must look at yourself three times as much as you look at your spouse. Rather than focus on the spec in your partner's eye, you should focus on the plank in your own.

As humans, we have a total of three core relationships that must be properly navigated and mastered. First, there is the relationship we have with God. It represents our vertical relationship. Second, there is the relationship we have with ourselves. It represents our internal relationship. Third, there is the relationship we have with our spouse. It represents our horizontal relationship. In order to have a fulfilling horizontal relationship, we must first focus on enhancing the other two relationships. As we work with God to become the best version of ourselves, our mates become more motivated to stay involved and emulate our behavior. By taking responsibility for your own actions, you demonstrate your commitment to the security of the relationship. By putting the spotlight on yourself and exposing your own faults and weaknesses, you encourage your partner to do the same. Don't do this as an attempt to change your mate, do it for yourself.

When my clients are truly ready to change, I take them through a comprehensive three step process. When asked, "Will it work?" my response is always the same. "It will work if you work it."

Step 1: Take Back Your Power

"Until you change the way you view your present reality, any change you experience will be haphazard. You have to overhaul your thinking about why things happen in order to produce lasting outcomes. It requires that you accept a new interpretation of what is real and true."

Now, read those words from author Joe Dispenza again slowly, focusing on the underlined words for emphasis- I don't want you to miss anything:

"Until you change the way you view your present reality, any change you experience will be haphazard. You have to overhaul your thinking about why things happen in order to produce lasting outcomes. It requires that you accept a new interpretation of what is real and true."

What a powerful statement. It implies that a mental paradigm shift must take place for real, lasting change. We can no longer blame others for our circumstances or make them responsible for our happiness. If we do, we give away our power, making them one hundred percent responsible for our present and future reality. According to the law of seedtime and harvest (cause and effect), our current reality is a result of the good and/or bad decisions we've made in our lives.

It's easy to blame our parents, the government, 'the man', our co-workers, the boss, the pastor, and our spouse for all the problems we face in our lives. However, the hard truth is, we are one hundred percent responsible for who and where we are in our lives. Whatever we experience on a daily basis, we've created it. If we're broke, we've created it. If we're overweight, we've created it. If we're suffering emotionally, we've created it. We have created every circumstance in our lives, either by our willful participation or our voluntary acceptance of something we knew wasn't in our best interest. The moment we embrace this truth we take back our power. So, in order to experience true change, we must accept, believe, and confess the following statement: "My spouse is not my problem; my own shortcomings are my problem!"

Once we truly accept that, life changes forever. With this new perspective in mind, review the following four questions which are based upon the aforementioned statement by Dr. Joseph Dispenza.

1) What is your present reality? (List all the challenges, circumstances, hardships, situations, and undesirable results you have faced.)

2) How have you previously viewed, justified, or rationalized the reasons for your present reality?

3) Understanding that you have the ability to create your own reality, what is your new interpretation of your current reality?

4) What will you choose to think, feel, and do based upon this new interpretation?

If you take the time to reflect upon these questions, and answer them honestly, you are one-step closer to your personal breakthrough.

Step 2: Begin Your Own Life Review

Self-Awareness means having a clear perception of your personality- including your strengths, weaknesses, thoughts, beliefs, motivations, and emotions. It allows you to understand your spouse, how he or she perceives you, your attitude, and your responses to him or her in the moment. As you develop self-awareness, you are able to make necessary changes in your life. The following passages of scripture speak to the need for self-awareness in a powerful way.

"Keep a close watch on yourself and on the teaching. Persist in this, for by so doing you will save both yourself and your hearers." I Timothy 4:16

"For by the grace given to me I say to everyone among you not to think of himself more highly than he ought to think, but to think with sober judgment..."
Romans 12:3

"For if anyone thinks he is something, when he is nothing, he deceives himself." Galatians 6:3

As you see, God wants us to become the best versions of ourselves, so that we can have the best marriages possible. That is the objective of Couples Academy. In the very first session, we take all of our clients through a detailed self-discovery exercise, which lays the foundation for our continued work together. Let me walk you through one of those exercises.

Issue Pie

First, take out a piece of paper and draw a picture of a huge eight-slice pizza pie. Above the pie, write the words 'Issue Pie'. The eight slices of the pie represent current issues plaguing your relationship.

Then, identify and write down the most pressing issues you currently struggle with in your own life (sins, challenges, weaknesses, vices, personality traits, behaviors, etc.). Place each word or phrase within a slice of the pie. Your list may exceed or fall below the allowable number of slices. If your list exceeds eight issues, please write them down outside of the pie. I often have clients who identify twenty or thirty issues that are deeply embedded within them.

Next, prioritize your list by writing #1 next to the most important issue needing to be addressed and resolved. Continue the process of numbering each issue, by order of importance, until you reach the end. Just as you can only eat one slice of pie at a time, you can only focus on and resolve one issue at a time. When you overcome your most pressing issue, you may find that it is tied to another issue in your life that must be resolved. Taking the time to genuinely examine one's self is a major positive step for someone who lives in oblivion or denial.

Finally, find educational resources (the Bible, books, articles, etc.) that explain the issues, and ways to overcome them, in a comprehensive way. With the proper amount of reading, prayer, confession, meditation, practical application, and personal accountability, you can systematically remove each issue from your life once-and-for-all. I also recommend working with a professional, as it is the best way to get lasting results.

Now, I can hear many of you saying, "You make it sound so easy. I've been like this all my life. Change is hard. I'll give it a try but I'm not promising anything." This is the natural response most of us have when confronted with change, especially if we've previously attempted to change with minimal positive results. Don't worry; I'll address your concerns shortly.

Step 3: Get an Image of Who You Want to Be

If you want to change, you must embrace an image of your idealized self- a model that you can emulate, which is different from, and better than, the person you currently are. Just as you've taken the time to write down the issues that plague your life, you must also write down all the attributes you want to acquire.

Who is the person you want to be? What do you want to do? How do you want to think and feel? We secretly expect something different to show up in our lives, but we continue to think the same thoughts, perform the same actions, and experience the same emotions every day of our lives. Most would consider that the definition of insanity.

If you want something different for your life, you have to see it. You must close your eyes and get an image of the person you want to be. If you want to be faithful to your spouse, get an image of it. If you want to walk in forgiveness, get an image of it. If you want to be more affectionate, get an image of it. Then, imagine yourself doing what it is you want to do. If you think this sounds like New Age mumbo jumbo, think again. Joshua 1:8 clearly says, "This book of the law shall not depart out of thy mouth; but thou shalt meditate therein day and night, that thou mayest observe to do according to all that is written therein: for then thou shalt make thy way prosperous, and then thou shalt have good success."

Booooom! Now, that's a powerful word from the Word of God. It's clearly telling us to train our minds, both day and night, to see ourselves doing the things we desire. When we live our lives by this principle, it will result in marital success. The more you hold on to the image, and the more you see yourself behaving in a positive way, the more you believe it is possible for you. It builds your faith and makes you committed to the process of personal growth and self-development.

Step 4: Discover A New Way of Living

It is vitally important to know that change isn't haphazard. It is systematic and intentional. It requires unlearning what you already know, in order to learn something new. You must unlearn the old habits you've spent your life naturally doing, and learn something new that feels very unnatural. This is done through a process called *The Four Steps of Processing New Information.*

Step 1- Unconscious Incompetence-You don't know what you don't know.

In the early years of our marriage, Danielle often complained that I was very critical. Unfortunately, I was unaware of my behavior. I didn't know what, how, or when I was being judgmental. I was oblivious. I didn't know that I didn't know how to effectively communicate. I was unconscious about my incompetence in the area of communication. Does that make sense?

Step 2- Conscious Incompetence- You know that you don't know.

In time, I became aware of the tone, temperament, and choice of words that offended my wife. I still didn't quite know how to fix it, but I became conscious about my incompetence. It is during this step that change can begin. Once you become aware of something, the journey of transformation can take place, but knowing is only half the battle. That takes us to the next step.

Step 3- Conscious Competence- You know that you know.

I found books, articles, and videos on how to effectively communicate and express my concerns in a positive and constructive way. I made the decision that I would no longer criticize her. I became very careful and intentional every time I spoke to my wife. Rather than say whatever that came to mind, I took the time to think about and review my tone and choice of words before speaking.

I finally knew exactly what to do. I became consciously competent. It wasn't easy. To be honest, there was nothing natural or comfortable about it. It felt very robotic and mechanical. Admittedly, there were missteps along the way and I occasionally slipped back into my old patterns and routines.

Despite the setbacks, however, I remained committed to the process. Why? I knew that I was breaking the habit of being my old self in order to become someone new and different. The simple act of repetition is what allowed me to reach the final step.

Step 4- Unconscious Competence- You know and it happens automatically.

My commitment to the process of overcoming this issue allowed me to remove it from my life. I transitioned from consciously doing the right thing, to unconsciously doing the right thing. How does that happen? Repetition. The repetitive process of doing the right thing, again and again and again, made it easier each time.

My behavior was no longer intentional. It became instinctual. As you review your issue pie, you will discover that some issues will be easier to resolve than other. Regardless of how long or hard it may appear to be, your uncompromising commitment to the process will ensure your success.

The key to marital success is in knowing that we are the common denominators in our relationships. If there are conflicts within our marriage, we should first take a look within. If we become the change that we are seeking, we are sure to spend more time in marital bliss than blunder.

Couples Testimonial from
Shane & Jodie Dennie
Toronto, Canada

Hasani Pettiford and the Couples Academy came into my life at a time when I was feeling overwhelmed and lost. I knew my marriage had issues but I also felt I needed help to fulfill my potential and be happy with who I was. I had tried therapy before on my own and with my husband but it was always short term solutions and we never really connected to that mode of help. I literally remember praying for something that could help us get out of our cycle of extreme ups and downs. And honestly speaking Hasani was our godsend. I am a more confident me and my marriage is a happy thriving relationship. We have an amazing support in Hasani who we continue to meet with for mentoring and coaching in all aspects of our life. We are grateful for him.

Place Your Marriage On The Path To Fulfillment
With CouplesAcademy.org

COUPLESACADEMY
PUBLICATIONS

Appendix

101 Ways To Love My Husband

Love Your Husband Back Into Your Heart

Hasani and Danielle Pettiford

Happily married couples live longer and healthier lives by building intimacy and reinforcing their commitment to one another through loving deeds. Inside *101 Ways To Love Your Husband* you'll find simple things you can do to make your husband as happy and ful- filled as he can be, such as?

Softcover, Jacketed ISBN: 9781494910525

101 Ways To Love My Wife

Love Your Wife Back Into Your Heart

Hasani and Danielle Pettiford

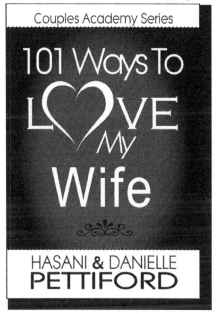

Happily married couples live longer and healthier lives by build- ing intimacy and reinforcing their commitment to one another through loving deeds. Inside *101 Ways To Love Your Husband* you'll find simple things you can do to make your husband as happy and fulfilled as he can be, such as?

Softcover, Jacketed ISBN: 9781494933074

Change Your Habits
Change Your Life
With 12 Steps To
Personal Transformation!

The 12 Habits of Healthy People This book will explore how to unlock your individual potential for personal health, fitness and nutrition.

The 12 Habits of Successful People This book will explore how to unlock your individual potential for personal greatness.

The 12 Habits of Wealthy People This book will explore how to unlock your individual potential for wealth creation.

Black Thighs, Black Guys, & Bedroom Lies

One of the most profound books on relationships
Hasani Pettiford

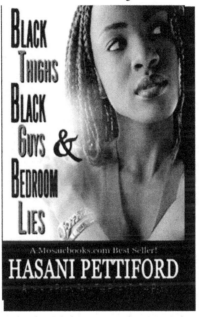

Black Thighs, Black Girls & Bedroom Lies is one of the most profound books ever written on relationships which clearly exposes how lust, deception and sexual self-gratification ultimately destroy both the individual and the relationship. Comprised of shocking information, statistical data and real-life stories, this hard-hitting message electrifies readers and fosters fundamental principles to help create positive relationships.

Pimpin' From The Pulpit To The Pews

A milestone book that will influence
a generation of churches

Hasani Pettiford

PIMPIN' From The Pulpit To The Pews is an explosive, eye-opening book that reveals how the spirit of lust has crept into the church and hs devastatingly affected both its leadership and laity. The book not only exposes the spirit of lust, but offers a step-by-step plan for overcoming sexual sin in order to pursue sexual purity.

Softcover, Jacketed ISBN: 09707915-1-8

Why We Hate Black Women
Discover Why We Hate Black Women and
Why We Should Love Them
Hasani Pettiford

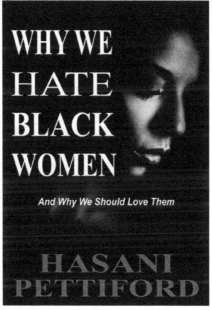

Why We Hate Black Women: And Why We Should Love Them is a book that takes a critical look at the lives of Black women in order to answer some critical questions: Why are so many black women alone? Why are they abused, abandoned, betrayed, devalued and hated? This quest for truth opens up a cultural Pandora's Box of issues that date back over 400 years.

Interested in hosting the Pettifords for one of their highly acclaimed live events? It's easy. Just visit www.CouplesAcademy.org to learn more and complete a speaking request form.

Hasani and Danielle speak to thousands of couples in cities across the nation and throughout the world. They are entertaining, insightful, and immeasurably practical.

"We have been going to marriage seminars for 17 years. The Pettifords, by far, provide the best presentation we've ever witnessed."
                                                              –The Howards

"Hasani and Danielle will revolutionize your marriage."
                                                              –John Williams

"Our partership with Couples Academy has helped save countless marriages in our ministry."
                                                              –Sarah Worthington

Learn more about the Pettiford's
"Audacity of Marriage Conference"
"AoM Virtual Experience"
and their
"Last Chance Weekend."

Made in the USA
Monee, IL
30 January 2021